TURNING IDEAS INTO RESEARCH

⑤SAGE | **50** YEARS

SAGE was founded in 1965 by Sara Miller McCune to support the dissemination of usable knowledge by publishing innovative and high-quality research and teaching content. Today, we publish more than 750 journals, including those of more than 300 learned societies, more than 800 new books per year, and a growing range of library products including archives, data, case studies, reports, conference highlights, and video. SAGE remains majority-owned by our founder, and after Sara's lifetime will become owned by a charitable trust that secures our continued independence.

Los Angeles | London | Washington DC | New Delhi | Singapore

TURNING IDEAS INTO RESEARCH

INTO

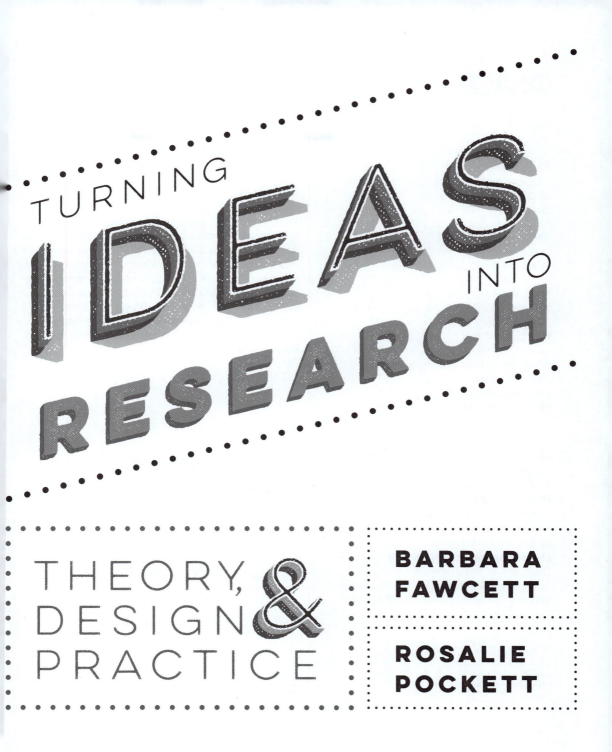

THEORY, DESIGN & PRACTICE

BARBARA FAWCETT

ROSALIE POCKETT

Los Angeles | London | New Delhi
Singapore | Washington DC | Boston

Los Angeles | London | New Delhi
Singapore | Washington DC

SAGE Publications Ltd
1 Oliver's Yard
55 City Road
London EC1Y 1SP

SAGE Publications Inc.
2455 Teller Road
Thousand Oaks, California 91320

SAGE Publications India Pvt Ltd
B 1/I 1 Mohan Cooperative Industrial Area
Mathura Road
New Delhi 110 044

SAGE Publications Asia-Pacific Pte Ltd
3 Church Street
#10-04 Samsung Hub
Singapore 049483

Editor: Katie Metzler
Assistant editor: Lily Mehrbod
Production editor: Ian Antcliff
Copyeditor: Richard Leigh
Proofreader: Sharon Cawood
Indexer: David Rudeforth
Marketing manager: Sally Ransom
Cover design: Shaun Mercier
Typeset by: C&M Digitals (P) Ltd, Chennai, India
Printed and bound by CPI Group (UK) Ltd,
Croydon, CR0 4YY

Library of Congress Control Number: 2014951037

British Library Cataloguing in Publication data

A catalogue record for this book is available from
the British Library

ISBN 978-1-4462-6670-0
ISBN 978-1-4462-6671-7 (pbk)

Contents

Researcher reflections

List of tables

FIGURE

Introduction

This book is about how to turn good ideas into viable research proposals and projects. Our purpose in writing it is to enable all those interested in undertaking research from a range of discipline backgrounds and practice areas to construct pieces of research that provide answers to the questions they pose. As part of this process, we focus on the research–practice interface and throughout we place emphasis on the real-world relevance of research and how to ensure that the research undertaken makes a difference.

Throughout the book, we develop three key themes. Each of these informs the content of each part of the book and the accompanying researcher reflections. The first theme refers to *world-views, understandings of knowledge and theoretical frameworks*, and here we acknowledge that these are vital aspects of carrying out any research project. Examining what informs research projects and what the overarching purpose is emphasizes the centrality of critical reflection and the examination of values. This ensures that the critical development of research questions that leads to the interrogation of knowledge remains a central focus.

Inclusivity and participation constitute the second key theme and bring to the fore the very important point that the era of researching 'on' research subjects is being replaced by a dynamic focus on researching 'with' research participants. This incorporates the need to pay attention to the power imbalances that operate both across the board and in specific contexts. Clearly the extent of participation and involvement will vary according to the project, but the placing of emphasis on these areas has now become a major area for consideration in all aspects of research, with these including the research purpose and the research design, as well as areas associated with interpretation, analysis and dissemination.

Our third key theme is *maximizing the impact of research in relation to 'policy to practice' and 'practice to policy' domains*. This recognizes that utilizing research within practice is not as straightforward as is often assumed. For research to make a difference in these complex contexts, we maintain that it is essential to take account of policy and practice frameworks by ensuring that research has policy and practice relevance. By highlighting the policy–practice interplay throughout the book we draw attention to detail, process and research impact.

In Part I of the book, we concentrate on *thinking about research*. Chapter 1 explores the many underlying reasons for carrying out research. We review different ways of researching and start to map out the connections between ideas, conceptual frameworks, the formulation of research questions and the devising of methodological frames. We also develop and take forward our key themes relating to the importance of world-views and embedded ontological and epistemological considerations, the need to prioritize inclusivity and participation, and the ways in which research can inform policy and practice.

Chapter 2 builds on the developing discussion and explores what is meant by partnerships in research and the importance of these in supporting and facilitating the impact factor of research. We discuss various styles and types of research partnerships and examine the reasons behind the forging of such partnerships. As part of this process, we take account of context and continue to look at the generation of ideas and how good ideas can be turned into viable research projects.

Chapter 3 explores understandings of ethics and how these inform the research process. This includes a discussion of the ways in which certain aspects are prioritized and others rendered less important. We recognize that the process of thinking about a project from an ethical perspective is a requirement but we maintain that there can be a disparity between where emphasis is placed and how participants are positioned in this process. In this chapter we also look at ethical decision-making based on ethical theories and perspectives, and examine the emergence of codified ethics processes such as professional codes of ethics and the place of research ethics committees.

Part II directs attention towards *thinking differently about knowledge and research*. In Chapter 4 we look at how to translate a good idea into a viable research project. At this point, we concentrate on the formulation of the research question and the mapping of the associated research design. We emphasize the importance of ontological position and how our view of the world shapes how we view knowledge. We then discuss the centrality of having a clear sense of purpose and consider matters associated with inclusivity in research. As part of this discussion, we also appraise the place of action-orientated research projects.

Chapter 5 is concerned with how to carry out research projects and we review and appraise qualitative orientations and the kinds of research approaches, data collection methods and data analysis techniques that can be adopted. In Chapter 6, we continue this emphasis and concentrate on quantitative orientations and the use of mixed methods. Chapter 7 highlights the importance of forms of evaluative researching. We recognize that whilst similar methodologies are used for evaluative researching and other forms of research, 'evaluation' is often seen to lack status. In this chapter, we review definitions of evaluation and the various ways in which evaluative research can be carried out. We also promote evaluation as a key method of research and highlight its importance as a legitimate research approach.

In Chapter 8 we turn our attention towards how to read research, how to take account of language and context and how to ascertain rigour and relevance. This chapter concentrates on how the context of the writing determines what is included and how this needs to be interpreted. This involves researchers locating themselves as critical readers and ascertaining the links made between purpose, analysis, findings and action. This critical interrogation is accompanied by a review of commonly used ways of producing research reports, and the chapter draws from relevant international examples to produce signposts and markers. We also look at evidence-based practice and the ways in which this broad concept has been put forward as the panacea for all problems experienced in social work and health services. Accordingly, we look at different conceptualizations of what constitutes evidence, the various types of evidence, its relationship with research, research rigour in relation to evidence and overall the utility of evidence in the arena of health and social work.

In Part III we look at the *impact of research*. Chapter 9 takes up this theme by looking at how all research carried out can make a difference. We explore ways in which this can be achieved, how research cultures can be sustained, and we examine strategies for the promotion and dissemination of research findings. We also discuss writing for publication and look at some practical steps and achievable goals for early-career researchers. Chapter 10 attends to impact by exploring the common pitfalls associated with carrying out research. It also focuses on ways of overcoming these by developing effective research supervisory relationships and building effective research infrastructures.

I

Thinking about research

ONE
Why do research?

In this chapter we look at the many underlying reasons for carrying out research. We explore different ways of researching and start to map out the connections among ideas, conceptual frameworks, the formulation of research questions and methodology. We also develop and take forward our key themes relating to the importance of world-views or ontological and epistemological frames, inclusivity and participation and how research can inform policy and practice.

Research and researching often acquire a certain mystery. Research activity can be viewed as requiring particular training, elevated skills or a proven academic track record. However, we want to start out by looking at research in its broadest sense in order to both simplify and emphasize 'doability'. We all can be seen to employ research skills in our daily lives as part of exploring an area where we need to gain more information, to check out something we are presented with or to question a statement or a position that has been adopted. Research is about wanting to know more, about working out how to do this and about exploring how action can follow from investigation. This is not to appear to dismiss research knowledge or training. It would be pointless to keep reinventing the wheel, but it is important to emphasize that we all, in various ways, engage in research as part of our daily lives and that we are all eminently capable of undertaking a variety of research projects.

Devising and carrying out a research project is often a question of confidence. If we believe we can do something then invariably we do it. If we doubt ourselves then it is all too easy to place research in the 'too hard' basket. There has also been an apparently impermeable barrier erected between researchers and students, between researchers and practitioners, and between researchers and consumers. If we do not feel able to carry out research generally or to look at those areas that we know about and have an interest in then we lose a significant dimension and leave room for others to constitute 'evidence' for us.

DEVELOPING RESEARCH IDEAS FROM PRACTICE

Context features significantly in relation to the undertaking of research. Politics, at national and local levels, exerts influence in terms of funding priorities, budgetary constraints, areas that are being targeted for investigation as well as a host of other aspects operating at a range of levels. Wherever a researcher or student is placed within an organization, the networking and resource opportunities available will feature significantly, as will the commitment of the university or organization. All of these factors can serve to govern the orientation of a research project, but whether there is a strong element of direction or whether there is more flexibility, research questions flow from the generation of good ideas.

In turn, good ideas flow from moments of inspiration, from detailed work in specific areas, from big-picture scenarios and from making links and connections.

It is also important to note that context incorporates current knowledge location in terms of contemporaneous influencing factors. Students, for example, will draw from previous experience, academic input and their discipline or interdisciplinary base to generate ideas for research. Those operating in fields of practice will have ideas associated with areas that are proving problematic or those which are working well. Coming up with a good idea initiates the research process and triggers commitment, enthusiasm and determination. A good idea may need considerable refinement to translate into a viable research question, as we see in Chapter 4, but without a good idea a research project will not get off the ground.

INCLUSIVE KNOWLEDGE BUILDING IN PRACTICE

Research can be undertaken as an individual activity and for many students resources and regulations can make inclusive and collaborative projects difficult. However, inclusion can now be seen to be featuring significantly in the arena of social research. Indeed, in terms of research making a difference to policy and practice, it makes sense to involve those in the change area, be they professionals, those who use services or, as is increasingly being acknowledged, those who wear multiple hats, in the process. Ensuring that 'end users' are included and participate in research is increasingly being recognized as a means of building capacity, and although, clearly, not everyone can be involved to the same extent, incorporating inclusivity as a matter of course into the design of a research project is now being taken on board by research funders as well as by those carrying out research projects.

However, it also has to be recognized that 'inclusivity' can be variously interpreted and it is not just a question of inviting everybody along; a great deal of thought has to go into making inclusion and participation work. This is an area we refer to throughout this book and specifically focus on in Chapter 2, where we look at partnerships in research, Chapter 4, where we explore turning ideas into viable research projects, and Chapter 7, where we consider forms of evaluative researching.

IDEAS AND THEORY BUILDING

In order to make sense of what is around us, we all develop theories. It is about posing 'why' questions, such as 'why is that person being responded to in that way?' or 'why are older people portrayed as "vulnerable"?'. Sometimes, what have been termed 'overarching' theories or 'grand' theories inform how we interpret and make sense of what is around us. Marxism and psychoanalysis are two examples of very different 'grand' theories which can serve to shape understandings and interpretation. In a similar way, modernism and postmodernism influence ideas, theory building and forms of analysis. Modernism, for example, can generally be regarded as encapsulating Enlightenment thinking associated with the supremacy of logic and reason over emotion and a belief in the march of progress. Postmodernism, in its embrace of uncertainty, relativity and fluidity, rejected the key tenets and securities of modernism, preferring instead to focus on contradiction, paradox and flux (Fawcett, 2000). We make meaning by theory building, be it by subscribing to or taking on board 'grand' theories or by posing our own theories to explain what we see around us. Ideas are about theories and ideas and theory building go together.

As part of this discussion, it is important to point out that scientific method and positivist traditions insisted that, in research terms, theories needed to be tested and proved or disproved by the application of prescribed methodologies. However, postmodernist influences have opened up the whole arena of theory building. This is not to say that in research terms 'anything goes' – throughout this book we point to the need for rigour in carrying out all research projects. However, we also want to highlight that ideas no longer need to be tied to particular positions, ways of operating or methodological frames. Researchers need to be clear about what has informed their idea or set of ideas and the theory building that has accompanied this and to present their case, but we want to emphasize that flexibility and creativity and innovation can be embedded in this process.

CHANGE AND TRANSFORMATION

As we have highlighted, all research has to have a clear purpose and all research involves politics at all levels. Although research can be undertaken in order to extend theoretical frontiers and to address gaps in knowledge frames, much research in the social field is orientated towards bringing about change. As Fawcett et al. (2010) point out, although the relationship between research findings, the production of 'evidence' and social change is labyrinthine, research has a vital role to play. It is also important to acknowledge that it is often the production of quantitatively obtained findings relating to, for example, unemployment, poverty rates, homelessness, and incidences of violence and abuse, that serves as a trigger for action, further research and change. As Fawcett et al. (2011) emphasize with regard to domestic violence, research focusing on prevalence has served to more accurately represent the extent of it and also to politicize the need for further research and action in this critical area. Similarly, the recent work of Marmot and the Commission on the Social Determinants of Health (2008) has thrown a different light on the factors associated with health and well-being globally and locally. Drawing clear links between health and the social circumstances in which people live, the health of individuals, groups and communities is no longer the mere absence of disease. Epidemiological studies drawing on quantitative methodology are now appraised through the lens of health equality and equity with a focus on the distribution of health resources. These debates have drawn attention to relationships of power and influence concerning the allocation of, access to, and availability of resources that need to be present to ensure that in its broadest sense, good health is within reach of all individuals, enabling them to lead a flourishing life (Bywaters et al., 2009; Wilkinson and Pickett, 2010).

Clearly, quantitative research projects involve the formulation of particular categories as well as the ascription of people to these categories. On the one hand, this can imply a degree of homogenization that does not exist; on the other hand, it brings to the fore findings that have the potential to change social policies and the practices of professionals who operate in the social arena. Overall, the utility of quantitative research processes in highlighting what is going on and in initiating transformation is of considerable importance, and we explore these areas in detail in Chapter 6.

This leads us to an initial consideration of the ways in which a mix of qualitative and quantitative orientations can effectively work together. Quantitative methodologies can produce data that draw attention to trends, patterns and frequency rates. Qualitative researching can utilize and drill down into quantitative data sets and, by means of an arterial span of analytical techniques from content analysis to discourse analysis, can explore insights, meanings and interpretations. This mix is both vibrant and productive, and we go on to examine a range of qualitative orientations in Chapter 6.

RIGOUR AND TRUSTWORTHINESS

Many new researchers want to carry out research into an area that they know something about or have a passion for. However, issues of bias and objectivity have tended to cause confusion for many, and in some cases have deterred practitioner researchers in particular from carrying out research projects. This confusion arises from the different ways in which qualitative and quantitative research projects are both conducted and evaluated. We discuss this further in Chapters 5,

6 and 8. However, debates about bias and objectivity have tended to come about as a result of the application of scientifically orientated positivist concepts to the social arena. This emanated from the belief that principles drawn from the natural sciences could be applied to the social world in order to uncover fundamental and enduring patterns and connections. Efforts to give social science the status of natural science initially forged this connection. This was underpinned by an emphasis on detachment, logic and the scientific formulation and testing of hypotheses. However, the view that there is an essential reality out there that can be uncovered by means of reliable and valid research methods that are applied objectively with mathematical and statistical precision has waned, and the influence of ontological and epistemological perspectives in quantitative as well as in qualitative forms of researching is generally recognized. Clearly, there are parameters to measure and assess the reliability, validity and generalizability of quantitative research and the trustworthiness and rigour of qualitative research. 'Scientific' notions of bias and objectivity associated with the more traditionally orientated positivistic traditions can be seen to have a number of limitations which have led to the association between quantitative orientations and positivism becoming much more flexible. This has opened the door to a greater number of research opportunities in relation to the generation of ideas and the formulation of viable research projects. This is an area we refer to throughout the book.

CONCLUDING REMARKS

Researching is a dynamic activity that enables researchers to manage complex networks, to move between different levels, to interrogate material analytically and to respond to dimensions of power. Researching also necessitates engagement with social, cultural, political and ethical agendas and facilitates the making of links and connections. Overall, in this chapter we have sought to draw attention to the breadth of researching possibilities. To return to the question of 'why do research?' we want to emphasize how research can make a difference, not only in relation to findings and outcomes, but also with regard to process. Researchers want to explore, investigate and analyse areas that they have a strong interest in and where they believe there are new developments to be made, new insights to be had, or where what is currently going on clearly warrants further exploration. Although, as highlighted, utilizing research findings is not as straightforward as is often assumed, research can make a difference in complex contexts by taking account of policy and practice frameworks and by ensuring that research has policy and practice relevance. We argue that illuminating the interplay between policy and practice serves to bring the detail and processes to light and enhances the eventual research impact.

TWO

Partnerships in research

This chapter reviews what is meant by 'partnership' in research and its importance in supporting and facilitating the impact factor of research. Various styles and types of research partnerships are discussed. Partnerships can be forged in order to review a common problem, or area for attention, they can take place between representatives of different sectors, and they can, importantly, include service users or consumers. Partnerships can also provide strategic opportunities for research funding, priority setting, idea development and the carriage of 'research agendas' that can sustain and support practice and policy development in the health and social work sectors. This chapter examines the importance of partnership in research and looks at how meaningful and workable partnerships can be formed and maintained. It also appraises possible problem areas associated with power imbalances and the operation of particular political agendas.

EXPLORING PARTNERSHIPS IN RESEARCH

The prospect of undertaking a piece of research from beginning to end is a daunting one – often so daunting in fact that many students and practitioners hesitate to pursue the development of good ideas into researchable projects. One manageable approach is to think about the research task through the lens of partnerships with others. Research partnerships occur when individuals come together in different ways to pursue research. This may include collaborations between researchers; relationships between researchers and all those engaged in the research process; and relationships between researchers and knowledge.

These three relationships will be explored in some detail, but they are by no means exclusive, as the research endeavour involves many fundamental relationships. In considering the initial engagement with research, Alston and

Bowles (2012) and D'Cruz and Jones (2014: 13) suggest that the identification of 'key players', and the answers to some specific questions, contribute to the initial work that must be undertaken by researchers to build both the conceptual and critical foundations of the project. These questions are: who is/are the researcher/s; who are the people being researched; what organizations are involved; who will benefit from the research; and who will be influenced by the research? The answers to these questions will also identify key relationships that exist beforehand or will need to be developed to pursue the research and the implementation of any outcomes.

Partnerships between researchers can take many forms. They can range from a simple partnership or collaboration with a colleague interested in the same area of inquiry about an aspect of their work, to very formal, contractual partnerships that involve significant research funding to study an identified problem or situation. For workers who lack research experience or the confidence to undertake an individual project, partnerships provide opportunities to learn from others; to learn together; and to affirm practice knowledge in the interpretation of data and the suitability of research design. Ideally, partnerships or research collaborations provide opportunities for the strengths and experiences of individual members to be shared and utilized for the common research pursuit.

In considering research partnerships, educational researchers Anderson and Freebody (2014: 5) state:

> when we use the term partnership research ... we are referring to a partnership between a researcher and a research context, and the people who associate with that context. Although classically in education, partnership research occurs between researchers and teachers, it could also involve partnerships with schools, government departments, community education centres, outdoor education centres, businesses or any organization concerned with education.

The expression of research partnerships in these terms can be used in many other fields of practice, including the health and social care sectors, and is a foundational component of new and inclusive ways of thinking about research, research orientations and the generation of knowledge. We will turn now to some specific types of research partnerships.

Academic-practitioner partnerships

Academic–practitioner partnerships are now a feature of the contemporary academic environment, with universities openly encouraging partnerships with industry. In the human services, health and social care sectors, collaborative and inclusive relationships have taken on distinctive qualities.

The academic–practitioner partnership draws on the strengths of each to complete the research. The expertise of practitioners is essential in informing the design of the study, enabling access to the sample group or data and the interpretation of the results. The expertise of the academic researcher is essential in the preparation of the ethics committee application, ensuring the methodological rigour of the study and the data analysis, and providing support in the final documentation of the studies for publication.

An example of academic–practitioner partnerships is where workers join an established research team within their workplace. Collaborations between social work and psychology within the cancer field have been significant in the developing discipline of psycho-oncology. In Australia, like many developed countries, funding for cancer research into the causes, treatment and management of the disease has been a significant priority of government for many years. Recently funding opportunities for research that involves bio-psychosocial approaches have been provided by organizations such as state-based cancer councils and cancer institutes. The interdisciplinary nature of these research partnerships has provided opportunities to explore both bio-psychosocial and inclusive and participatory understandings as part of the research process. The following example illustrates this type of partnership in the workplace. At a large metropolitan teaching hospital in Sydney, members of an interdisciplinary gynaeoncology team joined a practice reference group for a small funded study investigating the effectiveness of self-help groups as a support mechanism for cancer survivors and their families (Butow et al., 2005). The practice reference group included medical, nursing, psychology, social work and consumer representatives working in partnership with university academics who led the research. This group played an important role in the analysis and interpretation of data drawing on their practice knowledge and expertise. Their participation in the group helped develop linkages between practice, research and policy, and recommendations from the study were made to funding bodies to improve policy and practice approaches in this area.

The research partnership has resulted in further funding being received by the group for a range of mixed method studies, for example, Hodgkinson et al. (2007a, 2007b) and Hobbs (2008). A number of publications in refereed national and international health, psychology and social work journals encouraged all members to write for publication with authorship attributed in terms of the article development, the theme being documented and the journal to which the manuscript was submitted. The publication goals that were incorporated into the project enabled the trustworthiness and rigour of the studies to be assured through both internal and external peer review.[1]

---

[1]Information about the group can be found at its website: http://www.pocog.org.au/

---------------------------- **Researcher Reflection 2.1** ----------------------------

Thinking about research opportunities

To what extent are there opportunities within your workplace to join research teams as a practitioner member?

To what extent are there opportunities to develop academic-practitioner partnerships drawing on the research expertise of academics and the expertise of practitioners?

Within your workplace are there research initiatives currently under way that would benefit from the inclusion of interdisciplinary practice perspectives?

Are there policy-practice initiatives that might benefit from research from interdisciplinary approaches?

Student-supervisor research partnerships

Research partnerships and collaborations may also assist new researchers to develop a research reputation or 'track record' in a particular field. The domain of academic research provides a useful example of a scaffolded approach with higher research degree students working under the supervision of a principal investigator or supervisor. In this situation, students have made a deliberate decision to enrol in a postgraduate research degree to pursue a piece of research and/or to begin a research career. Even within the 'research nurturing' context of academia, the challenges in establishing a research track record and attracting research grants are recognized. Terms such as 'early-career researchers' and 'track record relative to opportunity' are common. The latter term specifically acknowledges that opportunities are hard to come by and may be restricted by occupational and personal commitments over and above the researcher's ability.

Opportunities for student participation in research can also be integrated into field education, practicums or placements within pre-qualifying and post-qualifying degree programmes. Illustrating a research learning opportunity for a student on placement in an aged care agency, Giles et al. (2010: 151–157) identify the research activities that were integrated into the student placement and the student's learning goals. These included understanding the policy and legislative context of practice and the service delivery demands of the agency; exploring various service models building on existing knowledge, skills and values; identifying approaches and theoretical frameworks for practice in aged care, critical reflection about their work and place in the research project and the development of research skills including running focus groups; analysing data and presenting research findings. Thus the research task was foundational to student learning on placement and not 'in addition to' the practice experience.

Research teams

It is uncommon for researchers to work alone. In fact, the more usual situation is for research teams to be formed that draw together a range of expertise to support the achievement of project outcomes. Research teams share common features with other workplace teams and can be understood in similar ways. Teams are groups of individuals who come together to work with each other for a common purpose. Small-group theory and theories about reflective practice and inter-professional working have informed the extensive literature on teamwork – for example, Brookfield (1995), Fook and Gardner (2007), O'Hara (2011), Reid (1997), Schön (1987) and Weber and Pockett (2011b). Feminist perspectives have also informed understandings of gender differences and the ways in which women work in small-group situations, and this has particular resonance for teams in the workplace including research teams (Schiller, 1997).

In a qualitative study exploring shared perceptions of effective teams, Mickan and Rodger (2005) identified six conceptual categories that were consistently present. These were mutual respect, goals, leadership, communication, cohesion and purpose, all of which were supported by 'active design and maintenance' (p. 367) underpinned by critical reflection and appraisal of performance, planning and evaluation. These elements interacted across four domains: environment, structure, process and individual contribution. Team functioning has also been represented through modelling team structures. For example, Pritchard (1995), cited in Weber and Pockett (2011b), described teams as being 'parallel', 'hierarchical' or 'collaborative', depending on team behaviour and characteristics around key tasks and activities. In parallel teams, disciplines work in parallel with each other and decisions are made independently with only occasional interaction, although they may be part of the same workplace. Hierarchical teams have a top-down approach to decision-making, and co-operation may sometimes be affected by power imbalances and inequalities between team members. In collaborative teams work is undertaken by team members with equal status and power, and close communication and shared responsibilities for decision-making are evident. Within all of these team models, difficulties will arise if there is a mismatch of purpose and team style or differing perceptions of them amongst team members.

--- **Researcher Reflection 2.2** ---

Characteristics of research teams

Compare your own experiences in teams with the criteria of effectiveness identified in the Mickan and Rodger study and the team models suggested by Pritchard.

Reflect on the characteristics of effective teams and consider the ways that research teams might ensure their effectiveness.

Research team members usually have different and complementary skills and expertise. These may incude theoretical expertise in the field of study; technical expertise in the development of research tools such as survey instruments and questionnaires; abilities to complete comprehensive literature reviews; interviewing skills; skills in data management, data analysis and data presentation; and administrative skills in negotiating and maintaining the infrastructure support required to keep projects moving forward to completion. As such they come together as a team of individuals who are no different from other teams in terms of how they need to function to successfully support their team purpose.

Processes need to be in place that enable team members to critically appraise and make decisions about roles and responsibilities. In the initial setting-up of a research team this may include agreements about intellectual property, recognition and acknowledgement of achievements, and publication and authorship conventions to be followed. Who will be first author, for example? What criteria will be used to determine first authorship: will it be alphabetical; by contribution to the content of the written work; or will all work be attributed to and led by the principal investigator? Roles for all team members need to be clearly articulated and agreed, including understandings of contributions and participation; regular and consistent communication processes need to be in place with clear documentation and reporting lines. Problem-solving processes need to be established, ideally based on a continuous open review and evaluation of all aspects of team functioning.

Teams can be interdisciplinary where members come together bringing different discipline perspectives, or unidisciplinary where members are from a single discipline. In interdisciplinary teams, some disciplines may be viewed as more powerful either by perception or assumed authority, and this is particularly the case when there is an already established hierarchy between those disciplines in the workplace. The health field is a good example of this where science-based professions are dominant. This may be further exacerbated on projects for which external grant funding has been obtained. Although this chapter does not address research funding specifically, it is true to say that competition for sources of research funding is universally fierce and the auspice of the funding body itself can also influence the way in which projects are developed. Funding bodies are 'key players' in the way projects are formulated (Alston and Bowles, 2012; D'Cruz and Jones, 2014). They are also a significant part of the research 'environment' referred to as a thematic domain by Mickan and Rodger (2005). The acquisition of research grant funding bestows significant status and prestige on research teams and, in particular, on the principal investigator. This can have a powerful influence on internal team dynamics, including authority and decision-making.

A further challenge in research teams is the dominance or privileging of research paradigms. In the health field, for example, the dominance of the physical sciences and scientifically orientated positivist world-views may pose difficulties for social scientists seeking to participate in blended or mixed method studies. The process of blending different research orientations together within fields where one has been traditionally more dominant presents a number of challenges. Appeasing dominant paradigms can sometimes lead to compromised methodology, as when quantitative approaches are applied to qualitative research design to meet more entrenched understandings of what 'good quality' research is. An example here may be the use of thematic coding software to analyse free text data that counts clusters of terms used by participants. Conclusions are then drawn from the statistical incidence of terms rather than the context in which they are used in an attempt to address a 'perceived bias' in qualitative thematic coding methods. Conversely, studies which are developed by teams drawing from qualitative research paradigms may make attempts to introduce quantitative elements to their study, particularly with regard to the findings where claims may be made that the findings have wider generalizability, when this in fact cannot be the case.

KEEPING THE POLICY-PRACTICE INTERPLAY ON THE AGENDA

As highlighted in Chapter 1, one of the challenges for those considering research is to think about themselves as potential researchers, thus breaking down the notion of a separation between research, work and practice. Most workers have the skills required to critically review and evaluate their practice, and this often occurs in collaboration with a more experienced worker in practice supervision. Whilst definitions of professional practice supervision vary, there are some common threads involving educative, administrative and supportive processes to improve professional practice (Kadushin, 1985; Davys and Beddoe, 2010). Professional practice supervision is a relationship through which these abilities are explored and nurtured; however, they are usually developed, honed and explicitly linked to the practice/work context. The appraisal of situations in this way can also lead to the identification of potential research ideas that could be further developed.

Similarly, those professionals who draw on critical reflection in their work can use this process to identify potential areas for research. Fook et al. (2006) identify key elements of critical reflection and reflective practice that include 'a process ... of examining assumptions ... embedded in actions or experience; a linking of these assumptions with many different origins ... a review and re-evaluation of these according to relevant ... criteria and a reworking of concepts and practice based on this re-evaluation' (p. 12). Critical reflection approaches in the human services field, in particular, aim to develop new approaches and understandings about practice, and workers can also use these approaches to develop research ideas.

Many workers engage in continuing education activities in their workplace as part of their ongoing professional development. Journal clubs and book clubs have been a traditional way to keep up to date with current literature about practice innovation. In extending to research literature, these small groups can assist in the development of research literacy. Finding common ground in both language and evaluation can be a useful introduction to the engagement and critical appraisal of research literature in partnership with colleagues. These groups can be led by workers themselves or can be in partnership with others, for example, academics from their own and related disciplines.

The small-group partnership, as a foundational activity for future research, has been successfully reported in a number of studies. Fouché and Lunt (2009) report on an academic practitioner partnership in New Zealand using a groupwork model aimed at 'strengthening research mindedness and research activity in social service settings' (p. 61). Similarly, Fouché and Light (2011) reflect on a small-group activity where participants are involved in 'a conversational process that helps groups to engage in constructive dialogue around critical questions, to build personal relationships, and to foster collaborative learning'. These examples present a model of engagement for practitioners, facilitated and supported by academic partners, that fosters relationship building as the cornerstone of future research partnerships.

The workplace and policy context of practice can often provide opportunities to undertake small-scale studies that aim to review or evaluate an aspect of the service. These are often good starting points for workplace collaborations. Let us now turn to an example to illustrate a workplace peer research collaboration.

A number of workers in a family support agency continually complain to their supervisors about the lateness of or failure to attend by some clients, blaming this on clients' lack of responsibility, inability to organize themselves and lack of respect for the service. Managers decide to undertake a small research study into the problem. A quantitative study is undertaken, gathering statistical data about attendance, lateness and failure to attend by clients. The results indicate that there are several repeat offenders and the reported problems have been verified or proven by the data collected in the study. One of the outcomes of the study is the recommendation to discontinue with some clients.

A group of workers interested in evaluative research who are also experiencing the problems reported, suggest to agency managers that another research study be undertaken using a different research approach. They suggest a review of the appointment-making process for clients, the waiting list and the reception desk experience of clients with and without young children. The project uses a range of different methods, including document analysis (agency documents/pamphlets about how to make an appointment and their availability in other languages); public transport timetables for accessibility; the availability of child care; analysis of the booking/interview schedules; observation; and experiential activities, that is, testing the process by stepping through it as 'a client'.

The results indicated a number of systemic difficulties for clients that resulted in their lateness or inability to attend, rather than their unwillingness to do so.

The results of this evaluative peer collaboration provided significant insights into the 'problem'. The study outcomes included a reconceptualization of the situation in a way that led to changes and improvements in agency practice. Following implementation of suggested changes in agency practice, an ongoing review was conducted which demonstrated that the problem was significantly reduced. No clients were discontinued from the service.

Researcher Reflection 2.3

Key players and stakeholders in research

Consider the 'key players' in this example and, putting yourself in their shoes, answer the five questions suggested by Alston and Bowles (2012) and D'Cruz and Jones (2014).

Who is/are the researcher/s?

Who are the people being researched?

What organizations are involved?

Who will benefit from the research?

Who will be influenced by the research?

Once completed, consider how do your answers differ for each stakeholder and why?

If another element in this scenario was that a majority of the clients were Indigenous people, we might further reflect on the world-view that this collaborative research represented. What assumptions have been made here about clients? What is the predominant story that is perpetuating a negative cultural perspective? From an emancipatory research view, Bessarab (2013) suggests that although well-intentioned, non-Aboriginal people undertaking research in the Indigenous domain require cultural supervision to enable them to look at different strategies that will work more effectively. In discussing a similar example she goes on to state:

> blaming Aboriginal people for not showing up at interviews or programs, or applying for positions, emerged as a routine behaviour of their practice. It is not until we unpack the why behind people not showing up or applying for jobs; reframing it within the context of power, history, race and control[,] that workers have been able to understand how they have been complicit in continuing to name the Aboriginal person as a problem, which is a loaded colonial construct that works to keep Aboriginal people powerless. (p. 88)

Some of these themes will be explored further in Chapter 7 on evaluative researching.

The pursuit of research relevance for practice has been one of the drivers in the emergence of the practice-based research (PBR) movement originating in the

United States and now an important example of practice-driven research partnerships. The work of academic researcher, Irwin Epstein, clearly demonstrates the trajectory and immediate adoption by practitioners of this approach to research (Epstein, 2001, 2009, 2010; Dodd and Epstein, 2012). In a deliberate repositioning of 'practice' preceding 'research', Epstein and others have developed a collaborative research model in which 'practitioners and researchers are full partners in every stage' (Dodd and Epstein, 2012: 199). According to Dodd and Epstein (2012: 15), 'PBR seeks to introduce research into practice in ways that accommodate to pre-existing practice considerations, values and ethics'.

One of the first significant studies published in the field was that of Zilberfein et al. (2001), a retrospective study of liver transplant patients at the Mount Sinai Medical Center in New York. The study also drew on the 'data-mining' technique of interrogating existing workplace databases as a research tool. PBR partnerships have since grown in reach and impact and have resulted in publications in refereed international professional and research journals by practitioners and academics (Joubert, 2006; Pockett, 2009; Pockett et al., 2010). Clinical data mining can be used by many disciplines: for example, Giles et al. (2011) published an innovative collection of studies undertaken by physiotherapists, occupational therapists, nurses, speech pathologists and social workers; physiotherapy researchers (Henderson et al., 2011) used clinical data-mining techniques to develop and trial codesets for diagnosis, priority-setting and assessing treatment outcomes; and in a study by Bone et al. (2011), speech pathology researchers used the method to explore voice abnormalities in patients with thyroid disease.

The development of practitioner research has followed slightly different pathways in Europe, Australasia and the USA. A comprehensive, critical review of this development has been undertaken by Shaw and Lunt (2011, 2012) and Uggerhøj (2011) who noted that practitioner research has been traditionally characterized by small-scale studies often focusing on aspects of good or desirable practice with underlying tension between it and university/academic research. Shared research and practice techniques such as reflexivity have provided a degree of common ground. They go on to comment that practitioner research in the USA has consistently drawn on scientific methods, with the prominence of intervention studies being a defining feature. We would suggest that the appeal of the PBR approach might also be understood in part as a response to these developments.

ESTABLISHING MEANING AND SUSTAINABILITY IN RESEARCH PARTNERSHIPS

Research partnerships exist with all those engaged in the research process, including research participants. In terms of the relationship between the researcher and those being researched, as we discuss throughout this book, there are some clear differences between the two key research orientations of quantitative and qualitative studies. These differences are discussed further in Chapter 4. Generally quantitative orientations aim to address elements of research reliability and rigour. Quantitative studies tend to be designed around a hypothesis, statistically significant sampling, prescribed methodology and statistical data analysis. Relationships between variables are determined by the structure of the research hypothesis.

Qualitative studies generally view those being researched as 'participants' rather than 'subjects' in the research process. Depending on the type of qualitative approach, there is usually a phenomenon or situation being explored or investigated that aims to increase the researcher's understanding of particular phenomena and experiences. In some forms of qualitative studies participants are actively engaged in the formulation of what is being studied, and, rather than there being a clear separation of roles, the researcher may become part of the phenomenon itself to further understand it. In these types of studies, research partnerships are inclusive and are based on equal relationships with knowledge and knowledge building. In her PhD research, Clarke (2013) illustrates this approach, stating: 'in this research project the interview is jointly constructed by the participant and the researcher'. She continues:

> Interviews within this approach become conversations between the participant and interviewer, with both being active participants in the interview process, jointly constructing the narrative that unfolds. Interview participants, and indeed interviewers, have multiple subject positions – not just one. This means there is not one identity waiting to be uncovered by the interview, rather subjectivities are contextual and local and multiple. (p. 62)

Drawing from two theoretical frameworks of poststructuralism and postmodern critical feminism and using narrative methodology, these relationships between the researcher, the data and participants inform the entire study, including the analysis and meaning-making of the research. Using another example, that of action research, the researcher becomes a facilitator in the process with others. The research aims to review, change and improve understandings of situations and experiences, and the outcomes of the study are implemented in an ongoing and integrated way. Potential and real power differences between those participating in the study are openly identified and actively addressed in the study design. All roles have equal value and significance in the research undertaking.

In Chapter 4 we go on to discuss the different meanings associated with participatory research, emancipatory research and inclusive research by using the example of researching work with disabled people. These differences are also particularly significant in research work associated with Indigenous populations. For example, in a study aimed at improving antenatal education for Ngaanyatjarra women in central Australia, and being mindful of the failure of previous initiatives, Simmonds et al. (2010) used a participatory research methodology in their study.

Key features included the establishment of a senior advisory committee selected by the women to oversee the study; equal contribution to the design of the study and decision-making at bush meetings of older women; and sharing traditional knowledge and practices with younger women and non-aboriginal staff (older women). The lead researcher was a trusted non-Aboriginal nurse and midwife accepted and known in the local community. These approaches challenge notions of researchers as 'experts' with associated positional 'authority' in the research work and are underpinned by epistemological and theoretical perspectives that will be more fully explored in later chapters.

The meaning and sustainability of research partnerships is underscored by researchers' relationship with knowledge, the development of new understandings and the potential to use this new knowledge for change. This foundational relationship will be explored in further chapters; however, we turn to it briefly here in terms of its applicability to the practice setting. In the earlier example of the interdisciplinary cancer research partnership, research outputs included the development of a quantitative measurement tool, the CaSPUN (cancer survivors' partners' unmet needs measure), that identified the longer-term supportive care needs of the partners of cancer survivors (Hodgkinson et al., 2007b: 805). A further study by this research partnership investigated the longer-term psychosocial outcomes and ongoing supportive care needs of gynaecological cancer survivors using a quantitative study design that included questionnaires and other measures (Hodgkinson et al., 2006). The hypothesis was that there was a correlation between distress levels and supportive care needs: that higher levels of distress experienced by patients would result in higher support needs. The findings in part indicated that 'comprehensive and extended supportive care services are required to address anxiety and trauma responses and investigate strategies to meet ongoing needs in order to improve long-term psychosocial outcomes' (p. 381).

These studies locate what is known and hypothesized within an empirical, quantitative frame. The identified needs and levels of distress are described in biological and psychological terms such as anxiety and trauma that indicate a need for psychosocial intervention or treatment.

Qualitative perspectives may use these studies as the basis for further exploration of the experience to gain a different type of understanding. This lens can make a significant contribution to the interpretation of the results and findings in such studies and in the design and carrying out of different types of studies that privilege the voice of the participants. Of further significance is the potential impact for change in wider systems, including government, community, agency and practice. In an article by the social worker on the team, Hobbs (2008) draws on her practice experience to identify two key groups of women who are diagnosed with cervical cancer. These observations form the basis of a different type of social understanding: 'Anecdotally, and at the risk of over-generalising, women with cervical cancer fall into two main groups' (p. 89). She goes on to describe the first group as younger women who may have a discovery of the disease in the context of childbearing and regular antenatal and post-natal screening. The second group is those with advanced disease who have not had regular and early access to screening programmes. Hobbs goes on to state:

> There are a variety of factors that mitigate against women accessing Pap test screening. These factors include, usually in combination, socioeconomic disadvantage; physical, intellectual or psychiatric disability; history of sexual abuse; family dysfunction; or simply being born in a country where there is no routine screening. For many of these women, the diagnosis of advanced cervical cancer is yet another disaster in a lifetime characterized by catastrophe, impoverishment, neglect and disadvantage; the sense of injustice here related not so much to individuals as to endemic social injustice. (p. 90)

These observations from practice illustrate the significant contribution to understanding the social experience in addition to the biological/clinical one and the possibilities of blended research approaches that inform each other, thus challenging any fixed views about incommensurability or the irreconcilable differences between research orientations and mixed method researching. Blended and inclusive researching can provide significant insights into the realities of situations, phenomena and experience that deepen understandings and contribute to knowledge building and knowledge creation. This in turn has implications for policy, practice and research.

CONCLUDING REMARKS

In this chapter, we have explored a number of key research partnerships that have relevance for practitioners, students and researchers. Key themes of participation and inclusivity have been explored in the theory, practice and workplace context. Specific examples have been used to demonstrate the ways in which fields still influenced by a scientifically orientated positivisitic legacy can be enriched by social perspectives of inclusivity and participation in research activities. Social researchers can be instrumental in bringing this knowledge to research collaborations that may not privilege it, and where other knowledge frames are dominant. Most importantly, these approaches in the social research arena push the knowledge boundaries beyond traditional parameters, leading in part to different and new understandings of the complexities of human and social engagement.

THREE

Ethical considerations

Contemporary expectations include the essential requirement that all research is conducted ethically. The formalization of research ethics can be seen in the growing number of national, institutional and agency-wide research ethics committees that set the parameters and foundations for research ethics approval. This chapter explores understandings of ethics and how these inform the research process. As part of this process, the ways in which certain aspects are prioritized and others rendered less important will be examined. Ethics is clearly more than a risk-management tool, but reductionist practices can serve to devalue outcomes. The process of thinking about a project from an ethical perspective is a requirement, but there may be some disparity about where emphasis is placed and how participants are positioned in this process.

In this chapter we will look briefly at ethical decision-making based on ethical theories and perspectives and the emergence of codified ethics processes such as professional codes of ethics and research ethics committees. We will then critically examine these in relation to contemporary research approaches of participatory, emancipatory and inclusive perspectives.

ETHICS AND RESEARCH

In considering ethics and research we must first consider the theoretical, historical and contextual positioning of the ethical bases of decision-making. Ethical discourses underpin the moral basis of decision-making. Put very simply, moral decision-making falls into two broad categories of theories that lie at each end of a continuum. At one end of the continuum are theories that are based on looking at the consequences of the action – decision-making is guided by the idea that an action or decision is 'good' because of its effects, for example, the allocation of a limited resource may be based on the idea of the 'greatest good for the greatest number'. This approach may be used in an emergency situation where resources are scarce, for example it underpins the decision-making in medical triage in disaster and medical emergencies. This of course means that some individuals may not receive treatment or access to the care or service; however, the decision can be justified on the basis of an ethical position about the consequences of the action.

At the other end of the continuum are ethical theories that are based on the intrinsic nature of the action – it is 'good because of what it is'. Philosophers arguing this as the basis of decision-making might argue about the sanctity of human life at all costs. The eighteenth-century philosopher, Immanuel Kant, espoused an ethical perspective based on understandings of 'duty'. This expresses our duty to each other as members of society.

Ethical philosophers can be located historically and contextually, reflecting the particular era in which their theories were developed. In doing so we understand that emphases and priorities of ethical positioning can be determined by the societal context of the day. For example, John Stuart Mill (1806–73) and Jeremy Bentham (1749–1832) espoused a utilitarian ethical approach, derivative of consequentialism (the greatest good for the greatest number). Utilitarianism privileges the benefits for the entire community over those of the individual. The mid- to late nineteenth century was an era of significant social reform, and this ethical approach to public discourse and provision helped make sense and give meaning to these social developments.

In contrast, in the postmodern era, feminist approaches, for example Gilligan (1982) and Noddings (1984), suggest that understandings of responsibility rather than duty, and relationships rather than principles, should be emphasized in ethical decision-making (Weber and Pockett, 2011a). These theorists posit that notions of 'duty' are in essence patriarchal and oppressive to women in that they place caring roles and relationships in the private rather than the public domain (Gray, 2010).

Another approach to ethical decision-making is based on the observance of four key principles that are so deeply understood in day-to-day relationships they are often taken for granted. The principles are: respect for autonomy; beneficence (or a duty to pursue the welfare of others); non-malfeasance (doing no harm); and justice (Beauchamp and Childress, 2001). A principles-based approach can be traced back to Hippocrates and the Hippocratic oath and its variations, taken by medical graduates to this day (Glannon, 2002). These four principles can also be identified as foundational elements of the codes of ethics of many other professions, such as social work (Banks, 2001; National Association of Social Workers, 2008; Australian Association of Social Workers, 2010; Weber and Pockett, 2011a).

The accepted hierarchy of these principles in Western societies places respect for autonomy and individuals' right to make decisions about their circumstances as carrying primacy over the other three principles of beneficence, non-malfeasance and justice. Although generally considered to be universally accepted, this is a contextual assumption that may be challenged in societies where the order of primacy of these principles may not be the same, reflecting different values and beliefs.

Hugman (2005) states that as part of everyday life, moral positions are taken and decisions are made by everyone. Much of this is implicit: people may not be required to give a reasoned account of principles when they make a decision about something that might be 'good' or 'bad', 'right' or 'wrong'. In the practice domain, ethics has underpinned the differentiation of 'professions' and professional practice from other occupations. Professions ascribe to codes of ethics that provide guides for professional ethical behaviour. Professional ethics is an extension of the ethics of everyday life but is different in that professionals must be able to analyse the ethical component of a situation logically, thus being explicit. The professional carries responsibility for this task and it cannot be delegated to others (Hugman, 2005).

Although aspiring to 'do the right thing' in all situations, the complexities and dilemmas of practice may result in the practitioner identifying more than one course of action that can be justified. It is in these situations, when limited assistance can be found in codes and guides, that practitioners' understanding of values and ethics becomes crucial. Ethical knowledge must be interrogated critically, providing a way forward for practice. The ability to reason and articulate an ethical position drawing on ethical knowledge and principles remains one of the hallmarks of the professional.

This same knowledge is the basis of the ethical stance taken in research ethics. It is only in very recent times, since the Second World War, that research ethics has been based on codified approaches. Research ethics as a specific field of ethics emerged in 1947 with the publication of the Nuremberg Code (US Department of Health and Human Services, 1949). This was in response to the atrocities inflicted on prisoners of war and those in concentration camps in the name of scientific experiments during the war years. Further developments in the decades that followed have resulted in universally accepted codes for ethical research. These codes are continually reviewed and updated to keep pace with scientific and biomedical advances under the auspices of groups such as the World Health Organization and the World Medical Association through the Declaration of Helsinki (World Medical Association, 1964).

The United Nations has also located ethical research practice as a human rights issue. Article 7 of the International Covenant on Civil and Political Rights says:

> No one shall be subjected to torture or to cruel, inhuman or degrading treatment or punishment. In particular, no one shall be subjected without his free consent to medical or scientific experimentation. (United Nations High Commission for Human Rights, 1966)

The history of these developments is mirrored in most countries in the Western world. Dodd and Epstein (2012) chronicle developments in the USA commencing with the Nuremberg trials in 1945, and several subsequent studies that were 'sentinel' in their failure to observe agreed ethical research principles, including human rights abuses, breaches of confidentiality and the absence of participant consent. Several of these studies have been well documented in the ethics literature, such as Milgram's Obedience Study published in 1974, the Humphrey tearoom trade study published in 1970 and the Tuskegee Syphilis Study protocol revealed in 1972 but begun in 1932 (discussed in Habibis, 2010; Dodd and Epstein, 2012).

Looking at two of these studies to illustrate these failures, the Humphrey tearoom trade study was a covert, ethnographic study of casual homosexual encounters in which the researcher actively participated as a lookout for participants. The researcher noted car registration numbers and about a year later contacted these individuals to interview them about their socioeconomic position. In a review of the study, Habibis (2010: 95) states: 'Humphrey's study challenged negative stereotypes about gay men and so made an important contribution to the destigmatisation of homosexuality. However its violation of fundamental ethical principles, such as informed consent, compromised its validity within the academic community'.

The Tuskegee Syphilis Study was conducted over 40 years (ending in the 1970s) and involved African-American men infected with syphilis. This study did not involve fully informed consent and, although providing some access to free medical care, failed to inform participants of their disease and failed to provide full medical treatment. These examples involved research with participants who were in unequal and powerless relationships with the researchers and who were from vulnerable groups, neither recognized nor acknowledged, at the time the studies were undertaken. The development and implementation of more stringent ethical research codes of practice that formally prescribed the researcher–participant relationship was a means of addressing the exploitation and abuse of well-intentioned research that impinged on and ignored both human rights and the observance of key ethical principles.

This is not to say, however, that a reasoned approach to ethical decision-making in research prior to the emergence of these codes was not possible. For example, if we consider a principles-based approach to ethics founded on principles that are considered to be deeply ingrained in everyday thinking and life, there has always been a means of reasoning out an ethical course of action. Given this perspective, we will now turn to consider some contemporary debates regarding ethics and research.

ETHICS, RESEARCH AND INCLUSIVITY

In returning to the concept of the relationship between ethics and moral decision-making, Hershock (2000) states that ethics is an expression of morality and can be understood in terms of the ways in which social relationships are envisioned at a given point in time. This has significant currency within the critiques of postmodernist thinking as morality is discursively constructed (Hugman, 2005; Ife, 2008). In speaking specifically about professional practice but making a point that is also relevant for researchers, Hugman (2005: 138) says that 'discursive ethics is the conduct of a dialogue about that which is good (values) and that which is right (actions) ... in which *all* those who are affected can participate'. This emphasis on participation is picked up further by Ife (2008). Although research ethics has been located within a human rights discourse, in critiquing this discourse, Ife argues that it is dominated by the voices of the privileged; a discourse 'of the powerful' such as academics, lawyers, politicians, religious leaders and so on about 'the powerless' (p. 136), that has resulted in well-intentioned but dichotomous positions. The dilemma is clear. Not locating disadvantage and powerlessness in this domain results in the exclusion and denial of human rights. However, the desired outcome, that of rebalancing privileged world-views, can only be achieved by full and equal participatory relationships. Extending these arguments further to the research domain, we can begin to see that codified ethical processes may perpetuate dichotomous positioning of the researcher and those being researched, even with the best of intentions.

The emergence of new and different research approaches has challenged the exclusivity of earlier research paradigms. These approaches have been iterative in their evolution and represent a repositioning of social research in equal partnership with research from the physical world. For the purpose of considering ethical issues, and although by no means fully representative of all types of research, the following discussion locates these as three waves of change occurring from the early 1970s to the present.

The first wave of change can be attributed to the emergence of qualitative methodologies in the 1970s that challenged not only the criteria used to evaluate the credibility of the research but also the fundamental ontological position regarding the nature of reality and the relationships between the researcher and knowledge. As qualitative methods found both a voice and synergy in the multiple truths and realities of the postmodernist era, the naturalistic paradigm became the frame of a broad field known as social research. Definitions of social research usually include reference to a systematic process or method of collecting information for the purpose of finding patterns or trends or new ways of understanding social phenomena or relationships. These understandings can lead to new ways of interpreting situations, meaning-making and actions; see, for example, Alston and Bowles (2012: 6) and Marshall and Rossman (1995: 15).

A second wave of change began to reflect the diversity and difference in social relationships that could be attributed to relationships of power. Emancipatory research became the means through which the powerless or disempowered could be privileged in the research endeavour not only as participants being researched but in the open acknowledgement and articulation of previously silent or taken-for-granted assumptions about situations and phenomena that were systematically discriminatory. Contemporary feminist researching can be located in this second wave. In both these research approaches, a variety of theoretical perspectives may inform the research design and interpretation of findings.

The most recent wave of change is the emergence of differing 'ways of knowing', which are particularly relevant in the field of Indigenous researching and also in disability researching. As part of emancipatory perspectives, these approaches challenge entrenched and systemic discrimination in the theory, design and implementation of research. Of significance to ethical considerations in these contemporary movements is the epistemological position of the researcher. In exploring changing ideas, Howell (2013), drawing on the earlier work of Guba and Lincoln (2000) and Heron and Reason (1997), examines various paradigms of inquiry and presents new commentary on this position. Unlike the accepted relationships that exist in scientifically orientated forms of positivist research, in constructivist and participatory methods a subjective relationship is developed between the researcher and participants. Findings are subjective, iterative and meanings understood in an interactive, inductive relationship that is not separate but a joined-up activity. This was briefly touched on in Chapter 2 when we began to explore the relationships between the researcher and knowledge.

In an example of the ethical tensions that these positions create, Morley (2011) has documented her experiences as a researcher using critical reflection as a research methodology. In a study exploring self-perceptions of failure in practice by sexual assault counsellors and advocates, critical reflection models developed by Fook (2002) and Fook and Gardner (2007) were used to explore dominant assumptions and discourses that implicitly disempowered individual workers in this field of practice. In a role that challenged the usual objective ethical positioning of the researcher, Morley was an active participant in the dialogue with research participants that led to a transformational view of the work being undertaken, actively challenging the assumptions of the workers in their descriptions of practice and experience. This position was supported by rigorous critical reflection, reflexivity and researcher supervision to ensure the trustworthiness of the study. In the study, Morley was also a participant, answering the interview questions herself and subjecting them to the same discursive analysis. In keeping with one of the principles of critical reflection and discursive analysis, artificial binary or dichotomous positions that become entrenched in subjective understandings of the realities of practice were broken down. Researcher and participants equally contributed to the 'co-construction' of knowledge. Morley concluded that this approach challenged the dominant view of what constitutes ethical research and in so doing was an enabling and emancipatory process for the participants through the shared, reconstructed discourses about their practice.

As seen in previous chapters, similar tensions exist in Indigenous research. Whilst external and objective ethical considerations are in place to prevent exploitative research processes, the relationships between Indigenous researchers and Indigenous knowledge cannot be subjected to what Bessarab (2013: 73) calls 'a colonizing, Western Enlightenment worldview'. She calls for the embedding of Indigenous epistemology in both practice supervision and research relationships. Australian Indigenous research contextualizes knowledge systems and ways of knowing through 'yarning', described by Bessarab and Ng'andu (2010) as 'a culturally safe way of engaging in conversation with Aboriginal people', and cultural supervision would be a key part of the relationship.

Even if the epistemological position of the researcher and the research draws on participatory approaches, this relationship with knowledge, that is, the co-production of knowledge through the research endeavour, is not automatically emancipatory. Drawing on extensive international work with refugee groups and internally displaced persons, Pittaway et al. (2010) and Hugman et al. (2011) critically examine the efficacy of such research approaches, the constraints and realities of work in the field, and the challenging organizational ethics processes. Their work suggests a new theorization of these relationships based on the work of human rights advocates, anti-oppressive social work approaches, a renewed emphasis on human agency and the privileging of reciprocity of benefit, with researchers being required to articulate clear and tangible benefits and outcomes for the groups participating in the research.

The ethical considerations here are clear and shift the emphasis and meaning of 'benefit' from that of an undeserved reward to explicit outcomes that lead to improvements and changes in oppressive social relationships. The challenge for research ethics committees is to ensure that they are open to these changes, ensuring that they assess whether researching is being undertaken ethically rather than to a prescriptive ethics formula. This may mean broadening understandings of the positioning of the researcher in the research; different ways of knowing and the co-construction of the entire research endeavour by both researcher and participants, including the development of the research questions; the theorization of knowledge; the research design and method; and the co-production of meaning and new knowledge.

ETHICS, RESEARCH AND TRUSTWORTHINESS

In considering trustworthiness, the nature of trust itself requires examination. Beauchamp and Childress (2001: 34) define trust as 'the confident belief in and reliance upon the moral character and competence of another person. Trust entails a confidence that another will act with the right motives and in accordance with appropriate moral norms.' Once again we can see the interplay of morality and ethical positioning in debates regarding the trustworthiness of research studies and their outcomes. We will discuss this in more detail in Chapter 8 when we look at the constructive appraisal of research and consider wider understandings of trustworthiness that include technical aspects that demonstrate trustworthiness in research orientations. Foreshadowing this, we can see that the nature of reality itself becomes the contextual arena within which research orientations are located. In scientifically orientated positivist orientations Lincoln and Guba (1985) suggested that the nature of reality is understood either as a single entity made up of observable parts and understood as one truth, or with naturalistic orientations where reality is multiple, constructed by context and meaning, and understood as an individual interpretation of experience. When these differences were being teased out, the place of values was also differentiated; however, some thirty years later, post-positivist research also needs to consider the value stance of research inquiry. Thus trustworthiness consists of more than a list of measurable criteria for methodology and research design.

UNDERSTANDING RESEARCH ETHICS COMMITTEES

Having explored the theoretical, historical and contextual dimensions of ethical decision-making, we can now turn in more detail to research ethics and the governance structures that have been developed to support, review and implement ethical approaches to research.

Research ethics has developed as a subset of wider ethical discourses that help us determine what are considered to be the 'right' and 'wrong' ways of doing things. They are based on values and beliefs that are held in high esteem and are aspirational to a society, a culture, groups and individuals. Most researchers and those thinking about undertaking research are aware of the societal expectation that research must be undertaken in an ethical way, and an important part of the research process is seeking approval from a research ethics committee. Many researchers, however, experience this process as yet another 'hoop' to jump through or even an obstacle to be overcome in their research programme.

Institutions such as universities, health services, government bodies and non-government agencies auspice and mandate research ethics committees to oversee the ethical integrity of research studies for which they are responsible. These committees usually operate within overarching national or state-based legislation and policy frameworks that adhere to and accept universally accepted codes for the ethical conduct of research. As previously discussed, they emerged in the 1960s in most countries in the developed world following international developments on the ethical conduct of research. Their main objectives are to review, approve and monitor research projects and investigations to ensure the integrity of the research and the welfare, safety and rights of those participating in it. They have powers to reject, sanction and terminate research activities that do not meet ethical standards.

These bodies are known by various names in different countries: some of the more common names are 'institutional review boards' (USA), 'research ethics boards' (Canada), 'research ethics committees' (UK), 'human subject ethics committees' and 'human research ethics committees' (Australia).

Research ethics committees usually have representatives from a broad cross-section of constituencies including biomedical sciences, physical sciences, humanities and social sciences, theological and consumer backgrounds. Research activity must be expressed in lay language and be able to be understood and assessed by members of the community as well as technical experts from the field who will determine its scientific and academic merit. Committees review research proposals in detail, and research can only proceed once their approval is obtained. When a study is completed, researchers wishing to publish their research in refereed journals or books are required to provide details of the ethics committee review and approval to editors.

With the emergence of these committees, predominantly in the mid-1960s, the criteria for review of research proposals was exclusively located within a scientifically orientated positivist research paradigm. The nature of reality was fixed, single and tangible. Research quality was measured by the adherence to methodology that measured elements, and quantified and proved causal relationships between identified variables located in a research hypothesis. Research studies could be trusted if they clearly demonstrated internal and external validity, reliability and objectivity. The researcher was independent of the research subjects. Research was done 'on' and 'to' subjects. Data and analysis were formulaic and context-free. The research was considered to be objective and value-free. Conclusions and results could be generalized and knowledge creation was linear, supporting one singular notion of truth and reality.

More recently, research ethics committees aim to ensure that relationships between researchers and those involved in the research process recognize and address implicit and explicit ethical relationships that may lead to the researchers and participants being unequal members of the research inquiry. This is particularly the case for groups that may be vulnerable to exploitation. In the case of research with Aboriginal, Indigenous and First Nation peoples, a further application may be required. In countries with Indigenous peoples, research governing bodies have developed specific guidelines for researching with them – for example, in New Zealand, the Māori Health Committee of the Health Research Council of New Zealand (2008); in Australia, the National Health and Medical Research Council National Statement Guidelines on research with Aboriginal and Torres Strait Islander Peoples, and the Guidelines for Ethical Research in Indigenous Studies (Australian Institute of Aboriginal and Torres Strait Islander Studies, 2012); and in Canada, a tri-council statement of the Canadian Institutes of Health Research, Natural Sciences and Engineering Research Council of Canada, and Social Sciences and Humanities Research Council of Canada (2010). These guidelines have been developed with and by Indigenous and non-Indigenous members, but are still considered by many Indigenous leaders as conforming to a white, Western, post-colonial paradigm (Bessarab and Ng'andu, 2010; Bessarab, 2013).

Although the governance structures of research authorities vary across countries, governments, universities, agencies and so on, there are some common elements of ethics applications that can be linked back to the ethical stance or approach that primarily informs them. In Table 3.1 we have identified some of these common elements with reference to the principles-based approach discussed in the earlier part of this chapter. Drilling down into each section, the four principles are clearly evident in the intention of each section.

Finally, ethics applications usually include questions about particular relationships between researchers and participants that may be considered unequal, and often list specific groups. Some relationships that may fall into this category are:

- Teachers and students
- Employers and employees
- Children
- Those in dependent relationships with government authorities, such as wards of the state and those under guardianship or care orders
- Prisoners
- Refugees and asylum seekers
- Members of the armed services
- Those with mental health issues
- Those with intellectual or developmental issues
- Patients and health care providers
- Aboriginal and Indigenous peoples

The intention of these questions is to clearly recognize that unequal relationships can exist between the researcher and those being researched. Research applicants who tick any of these categories on the application form need to satisfy the ethics reviewers that their research does not exploit or disempower these participants. The moral basis of such questions, their intention and possible outcomes are discussed later in the chapter.

In a few final words on ethics committees, we need to acknowledge the current reality for many such committees and the researchers who interact with them. The demands on institutional research ethics committees to review increasing numbers of research ethics applications each year, combined with the growing complexities of contemporary research approaches, have led to many of those involved in the process considering the possibilities of alternative methods of assessment and review. Whilst the established approaches have merit in the achievement of the ethical imperatives of these committees, without discretion they can at times be seen as prescriptive and counter-productive in terms of the spirit and intention of new research initiatives and more 'political' orthodoxies. Rather than considering the ethical merits of the study, there are, on occasion, elements of risk management and political pragmatism that may influence the levels of approval for some types of research. To many researchers the process of obtaining research ethics approval seems more a bureaucratic process than one about ethics. Conversely, for those who are members of research ethics committees, often reviewing underdeveloped and ill-thought-out applications, the process is a continual reminder of the need to uphold ethical principles and practices that are often poorly understood by researchers.

Table 3.1 Principles-based approach underpinning research ethics applications

Sections of an application to a research ethics review committee	Intention informing its inclusion	Ethical stance supporting its inclusion based on principles approach
Administration	Identifies those responsible and accountable for the study and establishes reporting lines, auspice and affiliation.	Justice/fairness through the open disclosure of the study in the public domain
Nature of research	An explanation of the type of study and the key methodologies to be used. Locates the research within a research paradigm that enables ethical reasoning to be applied.	Autonomy Non-malfeasance Beneficence Justice/fairness
Participants and recruitment	Establishes the relationship between the researcher and participants according to the research paradigm. How is the positioning of the researcher in terms of objectivity/subjectivity addressed? Is it appropriate, coherent and demonstrating an accurate understanding and application of the methodology?	Autonomy of participants in an equal relationship with the researcher
Privacy/confidentiality	Privacy ensures discretion and security of data-handling procedures including management, storage and disposal. Confidentiality ensures the anonymity of participants.	Autonomy of participants Non-malfeasance
Collection and dissemination of results	An explanation of data collection procedures and the open disclosure of findings in the public domain, for peer review and also to participants.	Non-malfeasance Justice/fairness in terms of the open access to information and the critical review of the findings and implications
Risks and benefits	Aimed at preventing exploitation, ensuring physical and psychological safety of researcher and participants; identifies benefits of the research for the wider community and the participants.	Non-malfeasance Beneficence Justice/fairness in regard to cultural competence; cultural knowledge and empowerment of participants

(Continued)

Table 3.1 (Continued)

Sections of an application to a research ethics review committee	Intention informing its inclusion	Ethical stance supporting its inclusion based on principles approach
Participant information and consent	Ensures that participants have a full and clear understanding of the study and what participation will mean for them. Withdrawal from the study without repercussions. In some types of qualitative studies consent may be ongoing and continuous.	Autonomy of participants in an equal relationship with researcher
Conflict of interest and other ethical issues	Can the trustworthiness and integrity of the study be assured? What is the degree of influence of any outside factors on the study? Does the researcher have competing or rival interests that may benefit from the results or findings of the study? Are there any relationships of personal gain?	Justice/fairness ensuring removal of any exploitative activities for personal gain. Conflicts of interest identified, implied or inferred must be fully disclosed and are taken into account in determining the veracity of the findings
Description of project	The research study is assessed on its theoretical, methodological and epistemological merits.	Autonomy Non-malfeasance Beneficence Justice/fairness
Field-based research and location	What provisions are in place to ensure that fieldwork adequately supports the aims of the project, the privacy and confidentiality of the participants; the safety of the researcher and the participants; the 'political' risks of research that may challenge dominant and prevailing orthodoxies; and cultural understandings in communities being researched?	Non-malfeasance Beneficence Justice/fairness
Declaration of researchers	The researchers are accountable for the study that will be undertaken according to the requirements and approvals of the committee. The research will be monitored through the submission of progress reports and any changes to the approved study will require further application to the committee.	Autonomy of participants in an equal relationship with researcher Non-malfeasance Beneficence Justice/fairness

CONCLUDING REMARKS

The process of thinking about a project from an ethical perspective is a fundamental activity that is integral to all research inquiry and not supplementary to it. Beginning from the accepted view that all research should be conducted ethically, we have briefly looked at the theoretical, historical and contextual positioning of ethical decision-making as a moral pursuit. We have examined contemporary understandings and perspectives, including the opportunities and constraints of formalized research ethics processes. In considering these ideas, we have undertaken a review of the developments in social research more generally; suffice to say that whilst these models are important for new researchers to understand, it is of equal importance to acknowledge that there can no longer be seen to be an absolute dichotomy between quantitative and qualitative methodologies or positivistically orientated and naturalistic paradigms. Critical theory, for example, has a place in post-positivism where mixed methods may be used and where forms of objectivity are still pursued, however qualified by the epistemological position of the researcher. These ideas will be explored in later chapters.

Inclusivity has been explored as a feature of contemporary approaches that challenge more privileged perspectives of the relationships between researchers, participants and epistemological positions. It is also suggested as a way forward in research ethics to counter well-intentioned but oppressively constructed research that may perpetuate systemic problems that the research is aiming to eliminate and the entrenched conceptualization of knowledge frames, towards a more emancipatory view.

II

Thinking differently about knowledge and researching

FOUR

Creating viable research from good ideas

In this chapter we look at how to translate a good idea into a viable research project, focusing particularly on the formulation of the research question and the mapping of the associated research design. However, an important starting point is to consider the importance of ontological position and how our view of the world shapes how we view knowledge, and this is what we will focus on in the first instance. We will then go on to highlight the importance of having a clear sense of purpose and consider matters associated with inclusivity in research. To illustrate this part of the discussion, we will look at action-orientated research as an example of a research approach that supports inclusivity and which can be undertaken by practitioner researchers, before moving on to look at turning ideas into viable research projects.

THE INFLUENCE OF ONTOLOGY AND EPISTEMOLOGY ON IDEAS

The way in which we view social issues influences how we experience the world and how we understand social relationships and interactions. The extent to which we reflect on our understandings and critique taken-for-granted aspects also has a bearing on how we interpret what is going on and how we incorporate this into our value systems. All research, including research taking place in the natural sciences, does not take place in a vacuum. Prevailing political, ethical, social and cultural contexts intervene, even in laboratories. What constitutes objectivity for one person may appear to another as a subjective position wrapped in an obscuring guise.

This applies to quantitative as well as to qualitative orientations. Even when logic, reason and mathematical formulae are applied to social phenomena, our personal and cultural value systems both affect and have a bearing on how we formulate categories. In this book we do not adopt a perspective which straightforwardly equates quantitative orientations with scientifically orientated positivist positions or erect a qualitative–quantitative divide. We clearly maintain that viewing the world in binary terms is an Enlightenment legacy which ignores complexity, uncertainty and the varied knowledge drawn from myriad experiences. Similarly, at the other end of the spectrum, adopting a relativistic position with concomitant instability and constant flux is equally unhelpful to the researcher. However, we do argue that world-view or the ontological position taken by the research or the research team is central to the research process. This also influences how knowledge is viewed and what kinds of knowledge are regarded as acceptable or unacceptable. These are matters that we consider throughout the book; however, we maintain that it is imperative to both recognize and consider the connection between ontological perspective and epistemological position. Often the two go together with values, social position, educational discipline area and situation informing how connections are formed; however, it needs to be recognized that there can also be a considered separation if, for example, a particular research project is undertaken for a specific purpose.

Overall, we maintain that where a researcher or student is coming from, together with their values and their knowledge base, has to be the starting point for any research, as does their recognition of this and their reflections on it. Clearly, a researcher may decide to adopt a quantitative orientation for a particular project, and this may not accord with their overall world-view. However, the point to make is that any researcher needs to question where they are coming from, what they want to do, how they are going to go about doing it and how the findings are going to be presented. We maintain that in order to produce useful research in the social arena, researchers have to operate reflectively and reflexively and to acknowledge that there are many different ways of knowing, all influenced by prevailing values and cultures. In a similar manner, and as will be addressed in detail in Chapter 8, with regard to the production of evidence, attention has to be paid to *who* determines *what* constitutes evidence and *where* the influences lie.

A SENSE OF PURPOSE

Turning ideas into viable research projects requires the researcher to spend time both thinking through the purpose of the research project and considering the associated meanings and perspectives. The posing of questions such as 'Why am I doing this?', 'What is the research for?', 'What do I hope to achieve?', 'What are the potential benefits?' and 'What understandings are operating?' is imperative if the research project is to achieve its aim. Fawcett et al. (2010) look at how research and strategic engagement can bring about both policy development and policy change. However, they maintain that in order to do this, it is necessary to establish the meanings and perspectives operating and to understand the range of political, ideological, social and academic lenses that can exert influence. They highlight the importance of research but also draw attention to the ways in which social policies are formulated under the influence of various, often conflicting, drivers. Social policy is viewed not as a rational, linearly orchestrated process, but as a constant kaleidoscopic interchange of interpretation, construction, interests, perspectives and orientations. In relation to purpose, however, they emphasize the ways in which research linked to different policy spaces can be flexibly utilized to bring about social change.

INCLUSIVITY IN RESEARCH

Research inclusivity is another area that we refer to throughout this book. The notion of inclusion can clearly refer to a number of different ways of working, with these being seen to stretch along a continuum with informed consent and the provision of accessible information at one end, to the full participatory involvement of all concerned in the research project at the other. In the social field, although natural science underpinnings can result in respondents or research participants being researched *on*, we view such practices with caution and foreground researching with. However, we also recognize that researching with, in turn, encompasses a variety of ways of working.

Feminist research methodologies in particular have taken forward the process of inclusive researching. Clearly, there are many forms of feminism and many forms of feminist researching. However, there are some common threads which reverberate across qualitative and also quantitative orientations, that have served to enhance inclusivity and promote deconstructive appraisals. These relate to three key areas: that aspects such as gender are not fixed and biologically determined but are learned social constructions; that the experiences of different women (and those placed into a variety of categories) have inherent value and validity; and that researchers must always be reflexive about the perceptions, knowledges, values and biases that they bring to the research process. These threads have considerable applicability to all fields of research. Research in the disability arena has additionally built on these key areas in the promotion of research inclusivity, and it is worth reviewing developments in this field at this point.

Moore et al. (1998: 12) maintained that

> research design moulds research findings. Any research which is based on an individual model of disability will inevitably recycle individual-blaming images of disabled people … Such research is invariably oppressive and sweeps aside the generic and collective interests of disabled people.

They emphasize that only research rooted firmly in a social model of disability discourse and practice, which addresses the ways in which people with impairments are disabled by a range of barriers, enables a human rights perspective to be given to issues which shape disabled people's lives. Moore et al. go on to state:

> Mystification of research objectives and techniques has, in the past, led to a neglect of personal experience in investigations of disability, encouraged projects which are irrelevant to those who are being researched and recycled oppression and ... marginalization of disability issues. (1998: 13)

They promote research between disabled and non-disabled researchers within an inclusive framework which has critical reflection on human rights as its foundation and which takes full account of experiential knowledge. They note how political and organizational frameworks and power dynamics, as well as the reification of the concept of objectivity, have been used to derail inclusive research projects, and they foreground the importance of not only agreeing at the outset how inclusion is to be understood, but also how this is going to be translated into action with regard to a specific research project.

Inclusive researching can be linked to but is not the same as emancipatory research. Emancipatory disability research has emerged from the disability rights/social model of disability movement and has built on emancipatory research methodology promoted by second-wave feminism. Emancipatory disability research has seven core principles which underpin a dynamic process. Utilizing the work of Barnes (2001) and Stevenson (2012), these can be seen to incorporate the following:

Table 4.1 The seven principles of emancipatory disability research (derived from the work of Stevenson, 2012)

Control: Disabled people must be fully involved throughout the research process, and non-disabled researchers have to be accountable to a research advisory committee run by disabled people.

Accountability: All research processes and practices have to be open and accessible, with the findings and implications being fully disseminated.

Practical outcomes: Research has to have the purpose of enabling disabled people to confront disabling barriers in practically orientated ways. It must not result in the exploitation of disabled people's experiences.

The social model of disability: Emancipatory disability research has to be underpinned by the social model of disability which focuses on how disabled people are disabled by social, political and economic barriers and not by individual impairments.

The problem of objectivity and the need for methodological rigour: All researchers need to clarify their ontological and epistemological positions and rigorously and publicly justify their choice of research methodology.

The choice of methods: The methods used have to take full account of the views of involved disabled people as well as the requirements of the project.

The role of experience: The importance of disabled people's experiences (which are varied and can be theorized from) has to fully inform the research project.

Stevenson (2012) highlights the difference meanings associated with 'participatory research', 'emancipatory research' and 'inclusive research' have to be fully acknowledged. Clearly, the emphasis can vary, but Stevenson's (2012) definitions are useful. She regards 'participatory research' as the active involvement of disabled people in the conduct of research and in decision-making processes. 'Emancipatory research' she equates with research being under the full control of disabled people, whilst 'inclusive research' she associates with a dynamic reciprocity between participatory and emancipatory paradigms. To give an example, Stevenson (2012) developed a form of participatory action research, based on the core principles of emancipatory disability research, which emphasizes inclusive action at every stage of the agreed research process. Working with young people with Down's syndrome, her starting point is that participation in the research project is as important as the findings, and by focusing on the operation of a circles of support project she links this to the citizenship of young people as well as to their personal goals. The resulting research question, 'What aspects of the Circles of Support project can assist young people in working towards the fulfillment of their personal goals as citizens?', can be seen to be practical, personal, participatory and action-orientated. Its purpose is to promote inclusivity and participation in every aspect of the research process.

As Beresford (2002) highlights, participation in research has both progressive and regressive potential. He argues that there are many models of participation, that the nature of participation in any research project needs to be critically and systematically reviewed, and that service user organizations and movements have to be integrally involved in the process. We fully acknowledge how concepts and processes can subtly shift from being participatory and inclusive to becoming reductionist and regulatory. However, the attention paid to research processes in the arena of disability can be seen to highlight pitfalls and strengths, and the experience and knowledge gained are eminently transferable to other areas. We acknowledge that high levels of participatory inclusivity may not be achievable in relation to all research projects. Nevertheless, we maintain that as a starting point all research has to fully take on board processes and practices which are non-oppressive, non-discriminatory and ethically sensitive, and that researchers have to be fully cognizant of the potential pitfalls.

In order to operate in this way, Smith (1990) and D'Cruz and Jones (2014) argue, with regard to both quantitative and qualitative orientations, that difference and diversity need to be fully taken into account. They talk about the importance of utilizing 'decolonizing methodologies' where difference and diversity are fully acknowledged and foregrounded. D'Cruz and Jones (2014) emphasize the importance of ensuring that research is not about the perpetuation of colonization and maintain – particularly in relation to research involving Indigenous communities, ethnic minorities and those on the economic margins – that research processes and methodologies must be continually interrogated to ensure that colonizing cultures are not replicated. They state that only by continually asking how we know what we know can research be regarded as trustworthy.

ACTION-ORIENTATED RESEARCH

At this point it is also useful to emphasize the utility of action research. This can be seen as a research strategy which builds change into the design of the research project. It focuses on collaboration between all those involved in the research process with findings being continually fed into practice scenarios, which are then subject to further research and evaluation.

Finch (1986) identified three key elements which can still be seen to retain current viability. These include:

- Action research having modest to far-reaching aims, where change strategies implemented on a smaller scale can inform larger-scale change platforms;
- Having a purpose of placing the knowledge gained in the hands of those who created it and who are most directly concerned in its effects;
- Having an egalitarian scope which in turn implies the democratization of knowledge and skills (adapted from Finch, 1986: 192–194).

Action research can be linked to practitioner research. This is where those working in an area carry out research into that area. Often this form of research is exploratory, looking at what is going on or examining the relationship of an outcome to an intervention or process. It is research which needs all to agree on a clear value base and to acknowledge that working collaboratively and in partnership requires a strategy to ensure involvement and degree of contribution. Action research can have a qualitative, quantitative or mixed method orientation, and there are still researchers who would argue from a scientifically orientated positivist basis that those involved in a topic cannot carry out research into that topic or area. We would strongly disagree with this view. As highlighted throughout this book, the notion of objectivity in the social arena can be re-evaluated by means of deconstructive appraisal. All research requires rigour, transparency, linkage between the orientation and the methodology and an evaluation of the overall study, but practitioner research has a valuable role to play in looking at what is working well and why, what is not working so well and why, how services offered are experienced by those using them and how organizational and managerial issues can affect what is on offer to the public. Clearly, there can be pitfalls. Management priorities can try to dictate a research agenda, particularly if work time is allocated. Similarly, there is no certainty that 'unpalatable' findings will be acted upon – although in any research this features as an issue. Additionally, research can sacrifice theoretical understandings to practice imperatives. However, to address these aspects, allegiances can be formed with research-active institutions, external mentors can be brought in, and research can be produced which places practitioners at the forefront of change and development activity, preventing a morale of reaction and cynicism.

TURNING IDEAS INTO VIABLE RESEARCH PROJECTS

The literature review

Ideas for research projects can come from a variety of directions. These can include social media, the media generally, coursework reading, work experiences, general observations, critical incidents and indeed any occurrence which gives a potential researcher food for thought. To take this idea further, it needs to be placed in the context of what has been written about this area. This involves scoping what is out there, looking for other research, if any, that has been conducted on this topic or on a similar one, examining the findings, appraising the strengths and shortcomings, identifying gaps and making connections with other areas. This encompasses searching library databases using Boolean search techniques, reviewing abstracts, using internet search engines as well as utilizing the bibliographies of relevant articles. These all form part of the literature review, which is an important aspect of any research project as it allows the potential researcher to assess the need for research in the identified area, to ascertain the viability and 'doability' of this, to explore the context and frame of reference, and to clarify both purpose and meaning. A literature review can also be used to formulate strategies about how to avoid the pitfalls that previous research has encountered and explore how to build on and add to research that is already in the public domain.

We contend that carrying out a research project can be seen to be like creating an entity out of a selection of apparently random pieces. This analogy works because there are lots of parts to fit together: sometimes there is an apparent but not an actual fit, and it clearly takes time to produce the full picture. A literature review assists in both taking forward the good idea, refining it into an overarching research question and justifying the rationale for proceeding with the research project. The subject also has to be clearly delineated, as for most areas there will be more material available than can realistically be included. All research can be regarded as an ongoing process of justification, and this is very evident in the literature review, where it is important to be as clear as possible about criteria to be included, criteria to be excluded and the accompanying rationale. It is also important to be critically and constructively analytical, investigating assumptions that have not been made explicit, drawing out different readings or interpretations, and constantly considering what is being presented in the light of the chosen idea and overarching research question.

All research projects need good ideas, but all good ideas have to be turned into viable research questions. How to do this revolves around the formulation of the overarching research question and the drawing up of a subset of associated interlinked and interrogatory research questions. As the whole research project revolves around the overarching research question and associated subset of research questions, a researcher needs to take time to get this right, and it is perfectly acceptable for there to be revisions as the research project progresses.

Overarching research questions linked to good ideas can be many and varied. Mason (2002) associates formulating research questions with addressing an intellectual puzzle, and she highlights distinct types of puzzles which a researcher may set out to tackle. Developmental puzzles set out to explore how or why something has developed. This can relate to attitudes (for example, attitudes towards asylum seekers); to ways of viewing a social phenomenon (for example, how and why mental health started to be viewed in predominantly clinical terms); and to the development and continuation of phenomena (for example, particular social systems or forms of government). Mechanical puzzles look at how something works or how an entity is constituted, such as the legal system or indeed personal relationships. This form of puzzle directs attention to why an entity works as it does. Lastly, comparative puzzles are concerned with concentrating on similarities and differences between particular areas. These can have an historical, contemporary or predictive emphasis. Accordingly, a researcher may be concerned either singly or collectively with what has caused two areas to develop differently, what has influenced the sustainability of this, and what is likely to happen next.

As Mason (2002) highlights, the puzzle the researcher formulates may be a version, combination or variation of these. However, the underpinning elements of all puzzles rely on 'what, why and how' questions, and these, as we have previously stated, are clearly linked to the ontological and epistemological position adopted.

Actually formulating the overarching research question from a good idea, in some instances, can be relatively straightforward. An idea linked to the best use of social media in schools, for example, could be turned into an overarching research question which asks 'How can social media best be used to inform the learning of students aged 14–16 years?'. However, turning other ideas into utilizable overarching research questions can be more complex. An idea linked to asset-orientated capacity building for older people in a specific community, for example, has to be framed in such a way that it is not too broad and too all-embracing. The number of different ways in which an area could be addressed also has to be taken on board. So, one overarching research question could be 'How is asset-orientated community capacity building understood in the community of Westcott and how is it manifested?'. Another research question could explore 'What aspects of community engagement in Westcott could be viewed as asset-orientated capacity building?'.

With regard to the drawing up of the subset of research questions, a key interrogatory device is to continue to ask 'What do I need to know and why do I need to know this?'. We contend that producing a subset of research questions serves to break down the overarching research question into manageable portions and militates against the researcher losing their way. To continue with the earlier example, the overarching research question 'How can social media best be used to inform the learning of students aged 14–16 years' could be broken down into the following series of research sub-questions:

- How is 'social media' defined in schools in the chosen area or areas?
- How is it used with pupils in the 14–16 age range?
- To what extent does this vary between schools in the chosen area or areas?
- What are the process issues that have been experienced?
- Do these vary between boys and girls in this age range?
- What are the outcomes?
- To what extent are these affected by gender?

These research sub-questions serve to maintain the research focus and ensure that any change in the research sub-questions is matched by associated changes to the overarching research question.

──────────── **Researcher Reflection 4.1** ────────────

Brainstorming good ideas

Brainstorm a number of 'good ideas'.
  Choose one and work on formulating a research question.
  Think about how this could be broken down into a set of research sub-questions.

Timelines and resources

Following the production of the overarching research question and set of research sub-questions, the next stage is to think about the proposed timescale. Drawing up a time line is imperative, as is carefully scrutinizing the resources available with regard to the activity required at particular points. Matching research activity to time frames and resources can appear to be an overly specific task to focus on in the early days of designing a research proposal, and it has to be borne in mind that this is a time plan that will be subject to change. Nevertheless, ensuring that ongoing attention is paid to these areas often makes the difference between a successful research project and one which falls by the wayside.

Research design

Ontological and epistemological considerations, together with the orientation adopted (quantitative, qualitative or mixed method), the refining of the overarching research question, the formulation of interlinked and specific research sub-questions and the literature review, form the backbone of the research design. These provide the links between the questions the research project is asking, the data collected, the analytical process and the conclusions drawn.

This leads us on to how information is going to be collected to address the overarching question and set of research sub-questions, and here the research design can be mapped out as follows:

Research approach

This relates to the choice of the research approach or approaches to be used. These can include ethnographic research, interpretative biography or narrative, discourse analysis, surveys, randomized controlled trials and so on.

Data collection methods

This involves a consideration of the best way to collect the information to address the overarching research question and subset of associated research questions. The method will relate to the orientation chosen and to the research approach decided upon. Examples of data collection methods include interviews, narrative interviews, participant or non-participant observation, questionnaires, and rating scales.

Sampling

Qualitative and quantitative orientations require different sampling techniques. These are looked at in Chapters 5 and 6, but at this point it is useful to note that quantitative sampling requires the application of statistical method, whilst qualitative sampling is more purposive and directed towards including participants who are likely to have something to say about the area being researched.

Data analysis techniques

Consideration must be given to the data analysis technique to be employed, and clearly this has to be linked into the research approach and data collection method. This area is explored in greater detail in Chapter 5. Qualitative orientations tend to employ a thematic form of analysis. There are many forms of thematic analysis, but one that is widely used has been developed by Attride-Stirling (2001). Her step-by-step guide develops thematic networks which facilitate the organization of data into basic themes, organizing themes and, finally, the overarching global theme.

In terms of quantitative orientations, a survey, for example, will collect data by means of questionnaires which will be either self-administered or carried out by means of structured interviews. The resultant data will then be analysed by means of the associated measuring tools, often using a software program such as SPSS (see Chapter 6 for more detail).

Evaluation of research process

Any study has to incorporate an evaluation of the research process. This is usually looked at in terms of what worked according to plan, what did not and what the researcher would do differently next time. This not only adds to the rigour of the process but also serves to take forward research in the chosen field.

Research dissemination

We focus specifically on this area in Chapter 9. Nevertheless, as part of the research design mapping exercise, it needs also to be included here. Research dissemination has to be seen as a vital part of the research process as it is the means by which the research findings are shared with the intention of influencing policy and practice in the chosen area. It can take place throughout the study and can include the following:

- Moderating e-discussion groups on emerging findings with interested stakeholders
- Presentations at key stakeholder conferences to discuss emerging findings
- Holding a half-day conference to share and discuss findings, process issues and recommendations
- Interim reporting, including the production of reports and summaries aimed at key stakeholders.

At the end of the study emphasis can be placed on:

- Producing a full technical report of the research project and its findings and learning
- Providing accessible plain-language summaries targeted at stakeholders involved in the project
- Holding a national dissemination to managers, practitioners, policy advisers and academics
- Producing a guide highlighting policy and practice issues
- Using multimedia (e.g. video presentations) to ensure accessibility
- Publishing research papers in practitioner, academic and policy journals
- Ensuring that a project website contains all the dissemination materials.

CONCLUDING REMARKS

Translating any good idea into a viable research question and research project necessitates effective mapping and attention to detail. Visionary thinking generates the idea, but systematic endeavour ensures that the research project is not only completed but also fulfils it purpose.

In this chapter we have looked at how to start to turn good ideas into viable research questions. In the next two chapters we will look at research orientations in greater detail and examine the range of data collection methods and data analytical techniques available.

FIVE

Designing a research project: qualitative researching

The refining of good ideas into research projects that are both viable and 'doable', as highlighted in Chapter 4, takes time. Ontological and epistemological reflection on the kind of world-view the researcher holds, or the stance that needs to be adopted for the purposes of the research, is crucial and informs the orientation of the research project in terms of the use of quantitative, qualitative and mixed method methodology. In this chapter we will focus on qualitative orientations and the kinds of research approaches, data collection methods and data analysis techniques that can be adopted.

EXPLORING THE QUALITATIVE CONTINUUM

Qualitative researching places emphasis on insights, meanings and interpretations. It is about exploring understandings and experiences and delving into the world of the everyday as well as into that which is unusual or out of the ordinary. There is a focus on particular contexts and on the investigation of nuances, depth and significance. Qualitative researching cannot be defined merely by perceived difference from quantitative researching. Neither can it be judged in quantitative terms with the focus being specifically on measures of reliability, generalizability and validity. Qualitative research emanates from a variety of intellectual positions and cannot be regarded as a unified set of techniques or philosophies. It is an orientation that has grown out of a wide range of intellectual and disciplinary traditions and, as a result, the process cannot be prescriptive. Rather the overall strength of this orientation lies in prioritizing the strategic significance of context and in interrogating understandings and explanations of the social world.

As Silverman (2000: 61) points out, initially qualitative ways of researching were often defined by means of a 'simple inductivism'. This was characterized by a belief that what was most important was for researchers to immerse themselves in the data in an unstructured, inductive and free-flowing way. However, this focus on description and representation soon gave way to a more rigorous approach. Although there remains a pronounced inductive element, as Silverman (2013) and Mason (2002) point out, in any qualitative research project it is crucial to start out with a loose working definition of what qualitative research should be. Drawing from Mason (2002) in particular, this includes:

> *Ensuring that qualitative research is systematically and rigorously conducted.* This is not to say that it should have a rigid or formulaic structure, as neither are appropriate. Rather that considerable thought, planning and systematic action have to go into the formulation of the research question, the research sub-questions and the overall research design.
>
> *Ensuring that the research is strategically conducted whilst retaining flexibility and contextuality.* This highlights that changes can occur whilst the research project is taking place and researchers have to be able to operate in a contingent manner.
>
> *The importance of reflexivity and critical reflection* in that both the project and the researcher's motivation and role have to be subject to ongoing critical scrutiny throughout the project.
>
> *Regarding qualitative research as an ethical and political practice* in that the research, however small the project, does not take place in a vacuum and has a wider significance.

Sampling

As highlighted in the introduction to this chapter, as qualitative researching does not look to generate validity, reliability and generalizability, statistical or random sampling does not feature. Instead, participants tend to be included on the basis of a purposive or snowballing sampling process which takes account of aspects associated with accessibility. However, both Silverman (2013) and Mason (2002) assert that qualitative research should produce social explanations which can be generalized in some form. One of the key ways in which this can be achieved is by 'theoretical sampling'. Silverman (2000, 2013) allocates three distinct aspects to this form of sampling. These are:

- Choosing groups or cases in terms of the pertaining theory. This relates to looking at generalizability in relation to theoretical propositions rather than to populations. It is about selecting groups or cases on the basis of their relevance to the research question or theoretical position and the explanation or account which is being developed.

- Choosing deviant cases. Although the choice of groups or cases is purposive, it is also important to seek out and include those cases which do not appear to support the theory being developed to ensure that the research does not tip over into the self-referential.
- Changing the size of the sample during the research. This is about ensuring that the research design has flexibility to take account of new factors that may emerge, or to concentrate on smaller or larger numbers of participants.

RESEARCH DESIGN AND QUALITATIVE RESEARCH APPROACHES

In this chapter we focus on a number of key ways of carrying out qualitative forms of research. These are not meant to provide an exhaustive overview, rather to provide signposts for researchers looking to take forward their overarching research questions. We regard the areas covered as referring to research approaches, but acknowledge that in some contexts some of these approaches could be referred to as research methods.

In the creation of viable research projects from good ideas in the qualitative as well as in the quantitative sphere, the choice of research approach is crucial as it in turn informs the choice of the data generation method or methods and the way or ways in which data are analysed. At this point we will explore the use of content analysis, ethnography, narrative biography and discourse analysis. However, we will begin by looking at the part played by case studies in the overall research design process.

Case studies

Hakim (2000) maintains that case studies are probably the most flexible of all research designs. This is obviously beneficial in that the use of case studies can be seen to facilitate creativity and originality, but there are difficulties also, inasmuch as case studies can be too flexible and lead to unclear and superficial methodological practices. Case studies can be used as a means of focusing attention on an individual transcript which can be interpreted as text, or an entity such as a school, organization, community or geographical area. Case studies comprise a research design frequently used by those adopting a qualitative or mixed method orientation; however, as Bryman (2008) points out, they can also be used as part of a quantitative orientation, although they may be referred to as a cross-sectional design. Overall, then, the use of one or more case studies allows an intensive focus on the chosen area and facilitates across case comparisons. Some researchers will identify their research as 'case study' research, whilst others will identify case studies as part of the process of organizing data collection or as a means of analytically interpreting the data.

Content analysis

Content analysis can be seen as lying at the quantitative end of a qualitative continuum. It is a relatively simple approach where, in relation to an interview transcript or text, a central theme is pre-identified so that the theme does not emerge from the text, but the researcher decides in advance what they are looking for. The central theme is then broken down into a series of analytical categories or key words or phrases and then the researcher counts each time these appear in the transcript or text. This can determine the importance attached to components of the theme, with importance related to the number of times a component is directly cited. Best (2012: 186) states:

> Content analysis is said to avoid the problem of interpretation because the emphasis is on what is said in the text rather than how it is said or in what context. If, for example, you wanted to identify the ideological stance of a politician, you could count the number of times a key word/indicator such as freedom was used in their election speeches.

As Best points out, content analysis is concerned with *what* is communicated rather than the intentions and motives of the communicator.

Grounded theory

Grounded theory focuses on a prescribed way of gathering data in order to generate theory. It is an approach developed and popularized by Glaser and Strauss (1967) and in subsequent publications. However, it is notable that Glaser and Strauss went on to develop the approach in different ways, with Glaser believing that Strauss (in Strauss and Corbin, 2000) was becoming too prescriptive and was placing too much emphasis on concepts rather than theories. However, grounded theory, as developed by Strauss and Corbin (2000), is about initially collecting data in a certain area without preconception. Explanation and theoretical development then follow a three-stage coding process comprising 'open' coding, which is about examining, breaking down, comparing and categorizing data; axial coding, where the data are put back together in new ways, primarily by making connections between categories; and selective coding, which focuses on identifying the core category or key concept which defines the account and systematically making and validating links to associated categories. Charmaz (2000) has made this systematic process more flexible by using open or initial coding, where emphasis is placed on generating as many new ideas or codes as necessary to cover the area under investigation as fully as possible, and selective or focused coding, where attention is directed to identifying the most common and revealing codes and generating new codes by combining open or initial codes. These regenerated codes are then used to re-examine the data.

Bryman (2008) asserts that grounded theory, in its varying forms, is more often honoured in the breach than in the observance and that claims of grounded theory being used are often made but infrequently substantiated. However, the basic tenets of grounded theory, where the researcher initially immerses themselves in the data and then, by means of a systematic coding scheme, conceptualizes or generates theory from the data, in many ways can be seen to encapsulate at least a substantial part of the quantitative analysis process.

There can be seen to be a qualitative data analysis continuum, with content analysis at one end, through sequential types of analysis (where words/phrases are initially identified, then grouped and regrouped to form major and minor themes), to more interpretivist thematic analysis (for example, the identification of common, organizing and global themes; Attride-Stirling, 2001) and at the other end detailed hermeneutically orientated analyses (such as that found in the various means of discourse analysis). However, a key difference is that grounded theory, in its various manifestations, claims to provide an all-embracing or comprehensive approach to carrying out a research project. This is in contrast to other forms of qualitative researching, where (apart from discourse analysis, discussed later in this chapter) choices are made about methods of data collection and techniques of data analysis.

Interpretative 'biography' or narrative

Research practices that encompass life stories and narratives can be looked at in a variety of ways and can be given many different titles. However, 'interpretative biography', a term originally coined by Denzin (1989), can be seen to encompass a range of approaches that variously explore how narratives can be constructed, interpreted and understood. Indeed, there is a wide spectrum with at one end Bordieu's claim that all biography is an illusion and represents the outcome of collusion between the narrator, the researcher and societal expectations, and at the other end narratives viewed as representations of reality which have a solidity and fixity which transcend context.

Interpretive biographies or narratives are used in research in a variety of ways. They can be employed to understand the connections between demographic descriptors and attitudes that relate to them, for example, street crime or immigration. They can be used as experiential stories which have the subjective power to question accepted practices and policies, and they can be employed to highlight social causationalist or social constructionist factors, such as the social determinants of mental health or how a particular individual came to be viewed as a miscreant or as a super-achiever.

Biographies or narratives are about individuals, language, experiences and interpretation. The general concept refers to the generation of a narrative that is free-flowing, uninterrupted and where the content, pace and style are determined by the narrator. It draws from a variety of orientations, including symbolic interactionalism, phenomenology, hermeneutics and forms of structuralism. There is accordingly considerable variation in how narratives are elicited and how the resultant texts are analysed. Rosenthal (1990, 1993) produced one of the best-defined methods and although this in turn exposed the methodology to the charge of being too prescriptive, it is well worth exploring her approach in more detail.

Rosenthal (1993) looks at the distinction between the 'lived' and the 'told life' and maintains that both become inextricably linked in the telling of the life story. Her view is that emphasis has to be placed not on what 'really' happened at the time, or on the accuracy of the reporting, but on the participant's present perspective and which selective principles have guided the choice of stories. While Rosenthal draws from the biographical interpretive method and, as such, is concerned with a full life story, other researchers are more interested in episodic accounts, and we will go on to talk about these a little later.

In order to generate the story, the participant – or, as referred to by Rosenthal (1993), the 'autobiographical narrator' – is asked, by means of an initial opening question, to give a full extempore narrative of experiences and events from their own life. The story that they give is not interrupted by additional questions, but non-verbal cues are used to encourage the narrator to complete their story. In a second interview, which takes place when the researcher has had time to review the narrative in detail, there is a 'period of questioning'. This is where the researcher asks questions on the narrative and on the topics and biographical events contained in the account. Attention is also paid to what Rosenthal (1993) calls 'blocked out' issues. These relate to instances where the researcher feels that something that should have been incorporated is left out.

Rosenthal (1993: 4) asserts:

> A life story does not consist of an atomistic chain of experiences, whose meaning is created at the moment of their articulation, but is rather a process taking place simultaneously against the backdrop of a biographical structure of meaning, which determines the selection of the individual episodes presented, and within the context of the interaction with a listener or imaginary audience. This texture of meaning is continually reaffirmed and transformed in the 'flux of life'. It is constituted by the interweaving of socially prefabricated and given patterns of planning and interpretation of the 'normal' life, together with the biographically relevant events and experiences and their ongoing reinterpretations. These reinterpretations are usually hidden from the conscious access of the biographer; they are constituted by the biographical overall construction – sometimes manifest in the narration as global evaluation, molding the past, present and anticipated future.

Rosenthal employs a hermeneutic case reconstruction as part of the thematic field analysis. Initially the narrative, now viewed as text, is subject to a biographical data analysis. Here all the information which can stand more or less independently of the narrator's own interpretation is taken from the interview and reviewed by the researcher in order to ascertain the possible meaning for the narrator. This is about reconstructing the actual chronology or the life history and placing these events in a life order. According to Rosenthal, this is about the reconstruction of the life story.

The second stage is concerned with the reconstruction of the life history. This is where the biographical data, extracted in stage one, is contrasted with the narrative and self-interpretations of the narrator. The aim is to try to reconstruct the biographical meaning which the experiences had at the time they happened.

The next stage focuses on a micro-analysis of individual text segments. Here hypotheses developed by the researcher are related to the meaning of experiences in the lived life history. This incorporates the overall biographical concepts and evaluations of the life story being checked and reviewed in a detailed analysis of single text segments. The purpose is both to check the hypotheses developed by the researcher and to focus on those aspects which remain unclear or insufficiently understood by the researcher.

The last stage is where the researcher undertakes a contrastive comparison of the life history and the life story. Rosenthal (1993: 8) gives an example:

> We have found out in thematic field analysis that the *Narrator* presents his life under the biographical global evaluation 'Since Stalingrad I opposed National Socialism'. Consequently he had all relevant experiences ordered and put in a way as if they all would have happened before Stalingrad (1943). However, the micro-analysis of a text segment leads to the interpretation that he still identified himself with the Germany Wehrmacht after the capitulation in 1945. Further the reconstruction brought forth his turning point and distancing from National Socialism only later in his time as prisoner of war. At this point of the analysis we are able to ask, which function for the biographer this kind of presentation has and further ask, which biographical experiences fostered this kind of self presentation.

As highlighted, Rosenthal's (1993) approach comprises interpretative stages. It acknowledges narration as a social construct comprising both social reality and the narrator's experiential world. As such it can be seen to occupy a space between narration as literal translation, and narration as a fluid and ever changing entity.

Researchers using interpretive biography or narrative tend to use a range of techniques and analyses and to draw widely from qualitative methodology. Allen (2001) utilized Rosenthal's work to develop a way of using this approach in a more episodic, but still structured way. He employed this methodology not to generally explore a life story, but to research a particular topic – tenants' experiences of housing renewal. It is useful to reproduce this here as an example:

Table 5.1 Interpretative biography or narrative: an example (Allen, 2001)

Analysis of Biographical Information

Identify all the facts contained within the transcript of the Narrator

Identify all the facts known about their life from other sources

Compare and contrast the two, paying attention to what is missing/extra/different

Thematic Field Analysis

Divide the conversation into sections by:

    Identifying when the topic being discussed changes

    Where the researcher has to ask a question that changes the focus to what is being discussed

As part of this process, examine what the topic of the whole section is

Look at each section as an individual component. Explore what it is saying in terms of:

    The topic being discussed

    The themes discussed within the topic

Formulate hypotheses in relation to the themes and topics contained in the narrative – does the answer to a question appear relevant? It is what would have been expected to come next? What does it signify about the importance of a topic to that individual? What does it appear to be saying about that person's view of self? etc.

Examine the sections as a sequence and as a whole conversation – how is the conversation structured and how does it flow? What changes as the conversation progresses?

Examine the topics and how these relate to each other – is there a consistent or differing picture as the conversation goes on? What do they say about that person?

Complete a summary of that topic for the whole conversation

Examine the themes – do these present a consistent picture throughout the conversation? What do they say about the person? Are there any overarching themes for that person or does anything stand out?

Complete a summary of each theme for the whole conversation

Overall Analysis

Look at the biographical information presented in the conversations – what is consistently presented and what appears only occasionally? What is the significance of this?

Look at the themes and topics in the conversations – which are repeated in each and which appear only once? Is there a consistency over time and what has changed? What does this indicate about the Narrator over a period of time?

Complete an analytical summary for each Narrator

Compare and contrast narrative analytical summaries

Researcher Reflection 5.1

Interpretative biography or narrative: An example

Ask a 'narrator' to talk about their experiences of a topic that links to your good idea translated into an overarching research question.

    Analyse the resulting account using the method described in 'Thematic Field Analysis'.

    At the end of this exercise, evaluate how useful it was in generating material relating to your overarching research question.

Ethnography

Ethnography is primarily about sense-making. It is associated with how those involved in any social interaction make sense of what is going on and how those researching and observing interaction interpret this process. It is an approach that can be used in a large number of settings, including virtual settings such as internet sites, with the primary focus being placed on the meanings that can be attributed to social action and on understanding the intention and motives of those interacting in any given situation. As part of this process, researchers try to place themselves in the social and cultural context of others so that they can reconstruct or re-experience the situation. The purpose is to understand those aspects which cause 'players' to behave in particular ways in certain contexts.

In order to fully understand what is going on, the researcher has to comprehend accepted social and cultural practices and has to stand inside the setting being investigated. As a result, authenticity is important, and Best (2012) emphasises that ethnographic research should take account of:

- The importance of providing complete accounts of the participants
- Avoiding oversimplification, ahistoricity and the suppression of information
- Refraining from overemphasizing or exaggerating points
- Not allowing ethnocentricity to colour the interpretations of the researcher

For some, an ethnographic approach is virtually synonymous with participant observation (Bryman, 2008), although for others ethnography can be a range of flexibly combined, but ethnographically focused, methods of data collection (Brewer, 2000).

However, there is general agreement that the researcher is involved with an individual or group in a way that allows them, by means of unstructured interviews, personal documentation, and forms of observation and participation, to gain information often over a substantial period of time. This then enables the researcher to interpret, again in a variety of ways which can include discourse analysis, what is going on. As a result, translating a good idea into a viable research question using an ethnographic approach requires the researcher to become immersed in the practices of a chosen individual, group or site. The emphasis on forms of observation moves the researcher away from a concentration on interviews or narratives and places them at the centre of what is going on.

However, there can be tensions associated with ethnographic approaches. Emphasis is placed on fieldwork, collecting information and spending time with the individual, group or groups being studied. This can lead to charges that the longer a researcher spends with the 'players' the more likely it is that their presence will influence behaviour and affect the outcome of the study. There are also ethical issues that can come to the fore, relating to how the data is collected and how open the researcher is about what they are doing. Some ethnographic projects, particularly in the past, have involved covert involvement by the researcher – for example, Patrick's (1973) study of a Glasgow gang. These practices breach ethical protocols of informed consent and also infringe privacy. As a consequence, with the application of more stringent ethical procedures by universities and institutions generally, covert forms of ethnographic research are now much less common.

Ethnographic approaches can be underpinned by versions of critical realism where beneath the layers of belief, cultural practices and contingency, the researcher sets out to uncover what is 'really' going on. Ethnographic approaches can also be informed by versions of discourse analysis. Here what is happening within a group is generally interpreted in terms of the production and reproduction of group reality. We will now go on to discuss discourse analysis in greater detail.

Discourse analysis

Discourse analysis can take many forms and be applied to many different mediums, including text, film and audio recordings. However, discourse analysis generally relates to adopting a deconstructive approach which is about taking apart what is there in order to explore underpinning knowledge, power and value bases and how these intersect in the situation under review. This involves focusing on the language used, the inflections, the emotions conveyed, the gaps or what appears to be left unsaid, the contradictions and the paradoxes. Within the various discourse-analytic techniques that can be employed, there is a recognition that there are lots of discourses operating and that there are no universal truths that can be seen to apply across time to everyone.

With regard to discourse analysis, as with other qualitatively framed orientations, sample size is not important. Potter and Wetherell (1987: 161) famously asserted:

> For discourse analysis the success of a study is not in the least dependent on sample size. It is not the case that a larger sample necessarily indicates a more painstaking or worthwhile piece of research. Indeed, more interviews can often simply add to the labour involved without adding anything to the analysis.

They go on to say (p. 162):

> There is a danger here of getting bogged down in too much data … the crucial determinant of sample size, however, must be, here as elsewhere, the specific research question.

Of all the theorists whose work has contributed to discourse analysis, the work of Foucault has been the most influential in relating concepts such as language and meaning to the operation of knowledge and power and to the formulation of discursive contexts. It is useful to look at his work in greater detail at this point.

Foucault's view of power differs markedly from a traditional view which sees power as being mainly based in legislative authority and codified in law. In this fairly standard view of power, power is regarded as being located in a particular area, or with a specific group, or viewed as a possession which some have and others do not. Accordingly, power is imposed in a predominantly hierarchical manner, with a variety of sanctions applying for non-compliance. However Foucault (1980, 1981a, 1981b) conceived a view of power which is both dependent on and operated by social relations and, as a consequence, is ever present. According to Foucault (1981b), power is not imposed but constantly circulates within the micro-practices of everyday social relations. To understand how power is operating, he maintained that all 'micro-practices' or relations of the everyday have to be viewed in their discursive contexts. By doing this, combinations of knowledge/power, language and institutional practices which inform what is generally taken for granted can be both identified and historically, socially and situationally located.

Foucault saw power as being intricately connected with knowledge. His view of how power and knowledge intersected and interacted developed and changed over time, but in later writings (Foucault, 1980, 1981b) he developed a form of critical enquiry which he called a genealogy of modern power. Foucault argued that the power relations which occur routinely by means of everyday social practices are those that matter. He maintained that although institutions reinforce power relations by upholding particular discourses (with discourses defined as regimes of truth sanctioned by regimes of practice), they do not create these discourses, but merely reproduce what is already there (Foucault, 1981b). Foucault linked genealogy to what he called 'eventalisation' (Foucault, 1981b). By 'eventalisation' Foucault embarked on a process of deconstructive critical analysis to show that what we take for granted has emerged by means of processes which need to be unpicked in order to understand how particular discourses became so influential. He linked eventalisation to genealogy by stating that both are about rediscovering 'the connections, encounters, supports, blockages, plays of force, strategies and so on which at given moments establish what subsequently counts as being self-evident, universal and necessary' (Foucault, 1981b: 6).

Foucault's conceptualization of how power/knowledge operate has proved influential in relation to discourse analysis and to the development of a range of interpretations. His work has influenced the development of poststructural and postmodern orientations and the development of deconstructive discursive methodologies which have had significant impact.

As part of this discussion, it is also important to note the contribution of what can be called postmodern feminist research to the development of thinking and research methodology in this area. Postmodern feminism has to be seen as a collective rather than a single entity, but the work of a number of contributors has explored how knowledge is positioned and legitimated with regard to power.[1] Flax (1992) contributed significantly to debates in this field. She examined the ways in which some knowledge claims have been positioned as lying outside existing power relations, resulting in assertions that such knowledge represents the truth and is therefore incontrovertible. Flax (1992) referred to power/knowledge claims represented in this way as being 'innocent' in that their authenticity appears unassailable. She argues that all knowledge claims, even those that we hold dear, have to be subject to a deconstructive discourse or postmodern analysis in order to analyse both how they arose and how they are being perpetuated. This, she contends, applies across the board with all power/knowledge claims, the dominant as well as the more marginalized or 'innocent' requiring critical interrogation.

Benhabib (1995) notably asserted that postmodern forms of deconstructive discourse analysis are incompatible with feminism, with feminism understood in modernist terms as a fight against oppression and discrimination manifested at a range of levels through a number of different mediums. This criticism is still at the heart of feminist debates today. However, this ongoing discussion draws attention to both a major strength and a potential weakness of deconstructive discourse analyses. The strength is that nothing is held sacred and all is subject to scrutiny. However, a weakness is that positions taken, particularly by those experiencing social, political and economic marginalization and discrimination, can be undermined, resulting in the dilution of social challenge.

There will always be detractors, as well as ardent proponents, of deconstructive discourse analysis. However, just as discourse analysis lends itself to various elucidations, so there are many discursive techniques for analysing text from a diverse range of mediums. However, it is possible to put together a flexible guide for those researchers undertaking this form of absorbing yet intricate analysis.

A rough guide to undertaking discourse analysis

Perhaps the first aspect to highlight is that discourse analysis can constitute an approach or a form of researching in its own right. Nevertheless, a researcher still has to produce their own initial good idea, convert this into an overarching research question (with sub-questions) and decide on the 'text' to be studied. The 'text' can be derived from empirical data collection methods such as interviews, focus groups or narratives, or from existing material.

Once the text (which can be a single entity, a collection or result from a number of interviews, focus groups etc.) has been identified, the deconstructive discursive process has to be both presented and defended. Different discursive researchers

---

[1]There are so many authors who could be named here, but a selection of 'founding mothers' includes Weedon, 1987; Butler, 1993, 1995; Fraser and Nicholson, 1993; Williams, 1994, 1996; Featherstone and Fawcett, 1995.

read texts differently, and there is a need to elucidate the process and to justify why it has been decided upon. However, areas which have been emphasized by a variety of authors (Macnaghten, 1993; Opie, 1993; Potter and Wetherell, 1994; Fawcett, 2000; D'Cruz and Jones, 2004; Grbich, 2004) are summarized in Table 5.2.

Table 5.2 A Rough Guide to Undertaking Discourse Analysis

- Pay attention to detail.
- Review the style adopted.
- Examine emotional tones and levels of intensity.
- Explore tensions, contradictions and paradoxes in the text.
- Review how power/knowledge frames are being both produced and reproduced.
- Identify what is being taken for granted and what is being argued.
- Look for recurring themes and patterned ways of presenting information or articulating experiences.
- Focus on what is not there as well as what is contained in the text.
- Pay attention to interpretative shifts. This relates to how material is developed or how a subject develops the account or interprets prompts.
- Analyse how social practices influence content.
- Consider how an individual/group is constructed in the text and in turn how they position/construct.

──────────────── **Researcher Reflection 5.2** ────────────────

Choosing a research approach

Reflect on your good idea translated into a viable research question and a set of sub-questions.

Choose a research approach (other than interpretative biography or narrative) and map out the data collection and analysis process.

Arts-informed research approaches

Over the last decade, arts-informed research approaches have gained prominence. These can vary from performance ethnography, where research into an area is presented as theatrical performance, to the analytical use of a variety of visual or multimedia forms. Cole and Knowles (2011) highlight that arts-informed research can serve as a methodological enhancement to other research approaches or can be used as a stand-alone research approach. An example of the former is where photographic and media formats are used to both supplement and enhance ethnographically generated life stories. When used as a stand-alone research approach, a variety of art forms, incorporating multimedia installations, live performance, visual narrative representation, music, video and photography, inform all aspects of a research inquiry from ideas generation to analysis and presentation.

Arts-informed research has a fluid and flexible format, and its utilization of a variety of art forms not only produces a powerful impact but also has the potential to reach and influence a broad-based audience. For some researchers, the elasticity and creativity embedded in this form of research may appear to lack rigour. However, Cole and Knowles (2011) argue that arts-informed research combines ingenuity, inventiveness, imagination and vision with a range of research parameters which ensure a flexible but robust methodology. They maintain that these research parameters include: intentionality or a clear intellectual and moral purpose; researcher presence, which incorporates both reflexivity and artistry; aesthetic quality, which promotes knowledge advancement through research rather than the straightforward production of an artwork; methodological commitment; holistic quality; communicability; and knowledge advancement, which includes theoretical as well as transformative contributions.

Data collection methods: interviews and focus groups

Although interview and focus groups are far from being the only methods used to collect qualitatively orientated information, they do tend to feature, perhaps to a disproportionate degree, in qualitative researching. Silverman (2004) highlights that 90 per cent of all social science investigations use some form of interview. As a result it is useful to look at these data collection methods in a little more detail at this point.

Research interviews are generally referred to as conversations with a purpose, and they can be conducted in a number of different ways, depending on the research question, the research design and the research process. Interviews are not exclusively the preserve of qualitative orientations and can be quantitatively structured, so that all participants are asked the same question in as similar a manner as possible in order to facilitate codification and statistical analysis. In qualitative interviews, although there can be a clear framework (sometimes referred to as a semi-structured format) to enable the researcher to cover the same areas with all participants, attention is directed toward individual experiences, the meanings ascribed and to sense making.

As Sapsford and Jupp (2006) note, the word 'interview' has many meanings. As a result it is often assumed that little pre-interview planning is required. However, as many researchers have discovered, how questions are asked has a strong bearing on the responses obtained. Influencing factors can include the manner and appearance of the researcher, the interview environment and the extent to which the researcher achieves a rapport with the participant.

Hall and Hall (1996) focus on practical social research and emphasize that interview planning is important. Whether an interview is going to be semi-structured or flexible and open-ended, the researcher has to think carefully about how they are going to obtain information to address their overarching research question. This will inform the nature of the questions posed and the extent to which these are going to focus on the experiences, emotions, meanings, values and underpinning knowledge base of the participants.

A researcher also has to devise an interview strategy and consider how to open an interview, how to close it, how to further explore areas raised, and whether to build into the design more than one interview or to leave this possibility open. There are also practical matters to determine relating to whether to take notes during an interview, whether to audio- or video-record the interview (with the attendant ethical issues) and how to provide feedback to the participant.

Researchers often find that their initial opening question and the story it generates or their series of semi-structured questions with or without more flexible follow-on questions will cause the participant to share previously undisclosed experiences or to revisit areas not thought about for a while. This can generate powerful emotions or result in the participant becoming distressed. The possibility of this occurring needs to be thought through by the researcher in advance and response strategies devised. In a similar vein, whilst the experience of the interview and the memories or emotions it generates can be valued by participants as a 'one-off' opportunity, other participants may want to further develop their relationship with the researcher, and these scenarios also require pre-planned responses.

Focus groups have been described as a tool for studying ideas in a group context (Morgan, 1997). According to Krueger (1994: 37): 'Focus groups involve homogeneous people in a social interaction … to collect qualitative data from a focused discussion'. As a data collection method, as with interviews, focus groups require careful planning and attention to detail. It can appear to be a good idea to bring a number of disparate people together to talk about areas relating to the research question, but without design and organization, the result can be a chaotic and possibly disjointed muddle which quickly veers away from the key topic.

Ideally, focus groups comprise between six and ten people with the composition representing a particular grouping, for example, those utilizing a particular service or those delivering it. Focus groups tend to meet just once, although follow-up meetings of the same focus group can be built into the research design. The meeting tends to last 1–2 hours and be structured to include one to two introductory or settling-in questions, two or three questions relating specifically to the research question and a summarizing or concluding question.

Clearly, there are practical matters to address associated with recruitment, venue, the timing of the meeting, whether expenses are to be paid or not and how the discussion is to be recorded. A significant amount of planning also needs to go into the management of group dynamics, and to use focus groups a researcher needs to feel comfortable operating as a group facilitator and moderator. This incorporates having strategies in place to return the group to the key questions if deviation becomes an issue, to handle dissonant voices and to ensure that the discussion does not dissolve into a series of fragmented conversations or become inaudible with a number of people speaking at once.

As with the analysis of interviews, transcripts of the discussion can be read and interpreted as texts or there can be a concentration on responses to previously identified topic areas.

This discussion of research approaches and data collection methods is not meant to form a comprehensive list, but to highlight both the differences to be found in qualitative ways of researching as well as to fire enthusiasm as to how the good idea, transformed into a viable research question, can be taken forward. All approaches lend themselves to particular ways of gathering data. Forms of grounded theory carry with them prescribed ways of collecting, interpreting and analysing information. Ethnography lends itself to various participant or non-participant observational techniques. Narrative or interpretative biographies are generally produced by accounts generated by means of an interview which use a general opening question. Discourse analysis concentrates on the hermeneutically orientated analysis of a text or medium, which can be produced in a variety of ways, including by means of an interview and arts-informed research combining creativity, artistry and methodological rigour and purpose.

The key point we want to make is that, in relation to the research approaches highlighted, data can be collected and analysed in a number of different ways and that for most there is flexibility, as there is with regard to the analytical technique to be used. The research design generated by the good idea and associated research question needs to be carefully planned and to be methodologically justifiable, but as part of this process, innovation, creativity and enthusiasm can play a significant part.

CONCLUDING REMARKS

In this chapter we have looked at ways of taking forward the research project, refined from the initial good idea, by adopting a qualitative orientation. We have discussed research designs and research approaches that can be usefully utilized. In the next chapter we will go on to consider research designs and approaches which follow on from quantitative orientations, and we also appraise the utility of mixed method research design.

SIX

Designing a research project: quantitative and mixed method researching

In this chapter we focus on the use of quantitative orientations and on combining both quantitative and qualitative ways of researching. There are a number of ways in which these orientations can complement each other and an example, which draws from a major evaluation carried out in the UK, is discussed later in this chapter. However, at this stage it is useful to look at quantitative orientations in more detail.

As discussed in Chapter 1, we warn against adopting a position where quantitative orientations are straightforwardly equated with positivist positions. Clearly, quantitative orientations have a historical basis in positivism, but we argue for the adoption of what can be called a post-positivist perspective. This recognizes the prioritization and application of standardized statistical tests as a means of demonstrating validity, reliability and generalizability, whilst also acknowledging that personal, social and cultural values influence both the world-view and ontological position of the researcher. We argue that where a researcher or student is coming from, together with their value system and knowledge base, has to be the starting point for any research, as does their recognition of this and their critical but constructive reflections on it. The point we want to make is that any researcher needs to question where they are coming from, what they want to do, how they will go about doing this and how the findings will be presented. As highlighted in Chapter 4, we maintain that in order to produce useful research in the social arena, researchers have to acknowledge that there are many different ways of knowing. In a similar manner, and as will be addressed in detail in Chapter 8, with regard to the production of evidence, attention has to be paid to *who* determines *what* constitutes evidence and *where* the influences lie.

Quantitative researching is about determining the relationship between facts and measures of reliability, generalizability and validity. These are backed up by established statistical tests which are seen as externally verifiable and are central to the methodology. Emphasis also tends to be placed on deductive and inferential reasoning processes. There are those who question the implied objectivity of statistical tests and argue that statistics operate as social constructs which arise from taken-for-granted ways of knowing. Accordingly, attention is directed towards critically interrogating how statistical processes operate and examining the underlying representations of reality (Garfinkel, 1967; D'Cruz and Jones, 2004). As a result, we argue that all knowledge claims need to be critically interrogated and that this relates to quantitative as well as qualitative orientations. Quantitative orientations have the capacity to organize data in ways which can contribute significantly to the momentum for change in public and social policy and associated professional practices. National census data, for example, is hugely influential and is collected by the Office for National Statistics in the UK and the Australian Bureau of Statistics in Australia. Similarly, at a global level, surveys and data collected by the Organisation for Economic Co-operation and Development and the World Health Organization are widely used in research studies.

Surveys can be used in a range of fields, for example the UK General Household Survey. In the field of nutrition, a survey reported by Nicholas et al. (2013) obtained information about the food provided to pre-school children that highlighted that although there had been a marked move away from snacks such as crisps, chocolate and fizzy drinks, the diets were still high in sodium and low in iron and zinc and in energy-producing carbohydrates.

One of the strengths of quantitative researching is the production of large data sets that can be appraised for the purposes of further research and policy development. These data sets are common in the health field, for example in public health and epidemiology and in the social sciences where surveys investigate, measure and quantify social attitudes. Examples of these types of surveys include the Australian Survey of Social Attitudes regularly undertaken by the Australian Consortium for Social and Political Research;[1] the General Social Survey in the USA; the German General Social Survey; and the British Social Attitudes Survey conducted by the National Centre for Social Research since 1983. We will consider the use of some of these data sets later in this chapter in the discussion of secondary data analysis.

The availability of such rich repositories of data, however, is not an end in itself. To use such data, researchers must pose research questions drawing on quantitative methods to systematically extract and analyse the relationships between selected variables that are the subject of the inquiry. In asking questions of the data, we would argue that the ways in which questions are posed is influenced by world-views and epistemological positioning. As an example we will explore the

---

[1]https://www.acspri.org.au/aussa

recent work of a small group of researchers in England (Bywaters, 2013; Bywaters et al., 2014a, 2014b) who have used research as a way of thinking differently about the challenging and very public discourse surrounding child protection responses. In a powerful opening paragraph in his first article on this subject Bywaters (2013: 2) states:

> On 31 March 2012, a child living in Blackpool, England, was eight times more likely to be 'looked after' out of home – to be in the care system – than a child in Richmond upon Thames, an outer-London borough ([Department for Education], 2012). This inequality in childhood chances exemplifies a pattern of difference across all English local authority areas which is systematically related to deprivation.

This situation is supported by evidence associated with measures of deprivation in local authority areas. Drawing on quantitative approaches, Bywaters reviewed the current evidence using existing data collections on child welfare services in England, correlated with the Index of Multiple Deprivation Scores (Department for Communities and Local Government, 2011a, 2011b). The research shows 'the clear relationship between a child's chances of being looked after or subject to a [child protection plan] and the overall level of deprivation in the [local authority] in which they live' (Bywaters, 2013: 8).

In this research Bywaters has asked questions of the data from a particular world-view that is positioned contrary to the prevailing discourse that is underpinned by neoliberal economic and social policies. Bywaters (2013: 2) argues that 'the exploration of *inequality* as a key concept in child welfare in England – or internationally – has scarcely developed'. Suggesting a different interpretation where child welfare is understood and acted upon by drawing on understandings of inequalities, Bywaters has argued that new ways of understanding child disadvantage beyond the child protection and 'looked-after children' (LAC) perspectives can open up the debate more widely. He goes on to suggest that local authorities in England no longer benchmark outcomes 'against their existing level of deprivation ... but ... break the link between deprivation and welfare outcomes by tackling deprivation and its impact on children's lives at the local level' (p. 13). Through a lens of inequalities, and drawing on the body of work concerning social inequalities, the effect may be to level up and make more equitable the resources needed to create an environment which supports families and children. Cross-national comparisons in this field suggest that this may also be a way forward in Australia where contemporary approaches to child protection in the last two decades have been focused on risk management and the removal of children into out-of-home care and more recently moving children into early adoption (Department for Education, 2011; see also the New South Wales Child Protection Legislation Amendment Act 2014[2]).

---

[2]http://bit.ly/1yLtoKu

This example is also illustrative of the work of Bacchi which we discuss in Chapter 8 when we consider the constructive appraisal of research where policy (and, we would argue, research) is determined by the identification of what the problem is meant to be.

Turning ideas into viable research projects directs attention towards research processes and research design. As we have seen in Chapters 4 and 5, once an idea has been translated into an achievable research question, issues of orientation come to the fore, together with the formulation of the research design and accompanying research approaches. Concurrently, the choice of research approach, as discussed in Chapter 4, carries with it accompanying data collection methods and data analysis techniques. In relation to quantitative researching, we will now look at a number of research approaches that can be utilized.

RESEARCH APPROACHES WITH A QUANTITATIVE ORIENTATION

Quantitative orientations rely on the use of formalized methods to describe what appears to be going on, to attempt to explain what is happening in terms of cause and effect, and to produce a range of measurements and statistical tests. As highlighted, these aspects can be influential, but equally, attention also has to be paid to the forms of measurement as well as the definitions to be used for the purposes of the research project. A researcher, for example, can look at how many women between 16 and 20 have been subject to a violent attack, how many young men aged 16 to 21 engage in dangerous behaviour and how many young people report experiencing an episode of mental distress in England during a stipulated six-month period. These are important questions where responses can inform policy and practice in a range of areas. However, findings can be influenced by how a 'violent attack', for example, is defined, by variations in what is regarded as constituting 'dangerous behaviour' and by the many representations of 'mental distress'. This means that researchers have to be as clear as possible about definitions, whilst also being aware that the resulting categorizations inevitably carry with them a reductionist element.

Validity, reliability, generalizability

As we highlighted in Chapter 1, these are all significant aspects of quantitative researching. Looking firstly at *validity,* this can be regarded as relating to measurement and causal aspects, with both being important and both having a significant role to play. There are clearly similarities between these areas, but there can also be a difference in emphasis. Measurement validity is associated with ensuring that we measure what we set out to measure. An example relates to researching into motoring offences using official aggregate statistics. If a high incidence of speeding offences is recorded during a particular period, for example, the question of what is being measured can produce a range of responses. These include: the number of speeding offences committed; the activities of police patrol cars; new legislation; and the influence of speed cameras. However, a strong degree of measurement validity can be established if attention is paid to the variables and if these are taken into account to the fullest possible extent. So, in relation to the example given above, aspects such as police activity and the introduction of new legislation have to be considered, the time of day needs to remain consistent, and the measurement criteria have to include the incidence of speeding on the same road before and after the introduction of a speed camera.

Causal validity or internal validity is related to establishing the effect of one phenomenon upon another whilst controlling for aspects that can influence the results. This means that the effect of A upon B has to be scrutinized in terms of additional influencing factors. If, for example, one school introduces a programme to increase healthy eating amongst children in the 5–10 age range and another does not, a comparison might show that the school with the special programme shows a clear increase in healthy eating whilst the other is found wanting. However, the comparison school may be in a high socioeconomic area where the levels of healthy eating are generally higher.

Clearly, both measurement validity and causal or internal validity are very useful measures. However, close attention has to be paid to ensuring that what is measured is what the researcher set out to measure for the purposes of the research project and that claims that A causes B are qualified to take into account a range of influencing aspects.

Generalizability and reliability comprise the other key aspects of quantitative methodology. These relate to two important but interrelated aspects. The first is the extent to which the findings can be seen to be statistically reliable, and the second the extent to which the findings from one study can be generalized to other population groups. An example of the latter is whether findings from a 'fear of crime' study carried out in one area can be transferred to another. Sampling features significantly in these calculations because the way in which the sample is chosen has a bearing on the overall generalizability of the findings.

Sampling

Sampling in its broadest sense relates to the selection of respondents for the research project to be carried out. Clearly, it would be impossible to include whole populations in research studies, so a sample or subset of the population is taken. This is where paying attention to the criteria of the study becomes imperative, with the study criteria mirroring the research focus. The size of the sample is also important, and this is where power calculations come to the fore. Power calculations are designed to ensure that the sample size is large enough to make statistical inferences.

There are two hypotheses which make up what is frequently referred to as the inferential statistical test. The first is the null hypothesis, and this predicts that the intervention or what is being tested will have a null or zero effect on the sample. So if a new home lighting product is being tested, for example, the null hypothesis works on the basis that there will be no change in the behaviour of the sample following their exposure to the new product. In contrast, the alternative hypothesis works on the basis that a difference will be found in the behaviour of those respondents in the sample following their use of the new product. The purpose of the statistical tests is to determine whether what is being tested or introduced has an effect on the respondents in the sample. Power calculations focus on having the optimum sample size to determine whether what is being tested or introduced has had an effect. These also look to ruling out what are generally referred to as Type I and Type II errors. Type I errors refer to an apparent difference, that is, a difference that appears to register but does not actually exist, whilst Type II errors refer to a difference that does exist but is not identified. Power calculations are used to determine an appropriate sample size and thus minimize Type I and Type II errors. This is achieved by ensuring that the power is at least 0.8. This means that there is an 80% or higher chance of a statistically significant difference being identified.

Power calculations require the use of a software program such as SPSS. Although these software packages require some additional training, it is the understanding of what power calculations are and their overall purpose that is most important.

Once an appropriate sample size has been determined using power calculations, further tests for statistical significance can be carried out. As before, these are about using additional statistical calculations to ensure that any changes relate to the test or intervention rather than to chance. This does not necessarily mean that the change is important, just that it is statistically significant. There are, however, further tests that can be applied to ascertain importance or effect. If a randomized controlled trial has been carried out, for example, with one group subject to the test or intervention (the treatment group) and the other not subject to the same test or intervention (the control group), the effect is worked out by calculating the difference between the groups. The calculation would therefore involve taking the mean or average of the group subject to the test or intervention and subtracting the mean or average of the control group. This would then be divided by the standard deviation (the measure of the distance of the scores from the mean or average of the sample). The extent of the effect is then related to the score obtained, with a value less than 0.1 referring to a trivial effect and more than 0.5 being seen as a substantial effect (Cohen, 1988).

As well as the size of the sample being important in quantitative methodology, the sampling technique used is also significant. The main sampling technique used for quantitatively orientated research projects is generally referred to as 'probability sampling'. This tends to take two main forms: 'random' and 'quota' sampling.

Random sampling has three main aspects. In stratified sampling, the population is divided according to aspects or strata such as gender, age and class. From each stratum a random sample is then taken, for example every 10th name. In multistage or cluster sampling, random subdivisions are made to render the sample more manageable. So, for example, electoral wards could be chosen at random, followed by polling districts within wards, then individuals randomly selected from within each polling district. Multiphase sampling refers to further sampling taking place, following the completion of a survey, for example. This could relate to a proportion of the full sample being randomly selected and further questions being explored.

Quota sampling is a form of non-random sampling where quotas from groups are identified on the basis of 'key' social factors, which can include gender, age, class, ethnicity and so on.

Any project utilizing a quantitative orientation also needs to take on board the relationship between independent and dependent variables as well as levels of measurement as these methodological considerations play an important part in shaping any research project.

A variable can be defined as an element or aspect to which different values can be attributed. The full array of values that can be attributed to any variable is commonly called a frequency or an empirical distribution (Bachman and Paternoster, 1997) and different variables will have differing numbers of values. For example, gender usually has two values (male and female), whilst age can take on a range of values. The distinction between independent and dependent variables is associated with the assumptions the researcher makes about the relationship between the variables. Whether a given variable is designated a dependent or an independent variable will fluctuate according to the overarching research question and the set of sub-questions being addressed. Overall, however, dependent variables are those that a researcher wishes to focus on in order to explain or predict an outcome. Independent variables are those that the researcher believes will bring about change in relation to the dependent variable. An example relates to older people and frequent admissions to hospital. Frequent admission to hospital is the dependent variable which may be influenced by independent variables associated with living alone, having a poor social network, limited economic means and so on. Independent variables can be viewed as a means of accounting for or explaining frequent hospital admissions.

Variables, to which a numerical value can be attached, are subject to four forms of measurement. These are referred to as nominal, ordinal, interval and ratio. Combinations of these four forms of measurement are often found in questionnaires. Nominal measurement or nominal scales produce responses by means of a simple coding frame. There is an emphasis on consistency and although numbers are used these are labels only and are not used in any statistical way. For example, in a questionnaire, respondents may be asked to give yes/no answers with yes being coded '1' and no coded '2'. In an ordinal measurement or scale, responses are ordered and assigned a value. So the coding for a Likert attitudinal questionnaire would be as follows:

Table 6.1 An example of a Likert scale

Strongly disagree	Disagree	Neither agree nor disagree	Agree	Strongly Agree
1	2	3	4	5

Interval scales rate results in terms of the score achieved, with results being rated at equal intervals. For example:

Number of Years Spent in Health and Welfare Services

Table 6.2 An example of an interval scale

None	1-5	6-10	Over 10
No. of responses	4	6	10

Ratio scales are used to depict variables such as age, length of time spent at an address and so on. A ratio scale measuring age would be depicted as follows:

Table 6.3 An example of a ratio scale

0-10	11-20	21-30	31-40	41-50	...
No. of responses	2	4	1	5	...

Cross-tabulations are visual displays of two or more variables (an example is shown in Table 6.4). This information can be presented in different ways using pie or bar charts.

The background of staff responding to the question 'Do an increasing number of primary school children have unhealthy diets?'

Table 6.4 Cross-tabulations showing variables

	Strongly Disagree	Disagree	Neutral	Agree	Strongly Agree	Total
Teachers	2	1	5	6	7	21
Health Workers	3	2	6	9	1	21
Social Workers	2	3	7	1	4	17
Educational Psychologists	4	2	6	1	1	14
Total	11	8	24	17	13	73

All of the above aspects are essential components of any quantitatively orientated research design. However, there are a number of research approaches, linked to research methods, which can be explored to translate the good idea, expressed as an overarching research question and subset of linked research questions, into a viable research project. An overview of these follows.

Data collection

Experimental social research

These research projects have the common theme of seeking to identify causal links between one factor and another and determining the extent to which one factor has an impact on another or whether changes in one variable produce changes in another. What has been called the 'gold standard' of experimental research is the randomized controlled trial. Randomized controlled trials focus on allocating individuals randomly to two distinct groups. The first is a 'control' group where individuals are not exposed to that which is being tested. The second is the 'experimental' group where members are exposed to that which is being tested. An important aspect of the trial is that individuals do not know to which group they have been assigned. These two groups are then studied at the same points in time both before and after the administration of that which is being tested and the results compared. Some trials incorporate a number of groups and vary the administration of the test. There is also the possibility of the two groups being systematically followed up over a longer period. The randomized nature of the sampling undertaken, the systematic collection of the data at defined points and the scale of the project in terms of the number of participants involved are all seen as essential components. Randomized controlled trials continue to feature significantly in medical research in particular, although the tension between ethical propriety (the acceptability of participants not knowing to which group they have been assigned and the individual implications of this) and scientific measurability remains an issue.

Secondary quantitative analysis

Secondary quantitative analysis is a form of data analysis that relates to a reanalysis of previously collected data. It can include the reanalysis of material collected by organizations, governments and administrative records offices in order to identify significant trends or patterns. The analysis of data in this way has recently been reinvigorated as a research approach for practitioners who wish to undertake research about their practice drawing on the data sets that may be available in their agency or wider practice domain. In Chapters 2 and 8 we discuss data mining and the work of Epstein (2001, 2009, 2010, 2012) in particular, who has reconceptualized the approach as an effective and 'doable' research strategy for practitioners about their practice, which draws on a range of established research methods. The foundation of this approach is secondary data analysis that has been widely used by quantitative researchers as a means of exploring and interrogating material that has already been produced, to generate fresh results. An example of this approach is a wide-ranging investigation of the distribution of disadvantage in Australia by social work researcher, Tony Vinson. Using existing data collections of federal, state and local authorities Vinson (2007: vii) was able:

to demonstrate statistically reliable and consistent information about every population centre in this country on more than twenty different disadvantage factors [and] also an analysis of that data which provides an insight into the way in which social disadvantage can become entrenched, if not addressed in an integrated way by government authorities.

The indicators of disadvantage that were systematically analysed were grouped into five key areas where data sets were routinely collected. The purpose of this study was to 'join up' the data that were already known and routinely collected by separate authorities to present a picture of disadvantage substantiated by the evidence of quantitative data. The five areas were 'social distress', where data were available concerning low family income, rental stress, home purchase stress and lone person households; 'health', where data were available concerning low birth-weight, childhood injuries, deficient immunization and so on; 'community safety', indicators of which included confirmed child maltreatment, criminal convictions and domestic violence; 'economic' indicators included data sets on unskilled workers, unemployment and low mean taxable income; and 'education', where data sets used included non-attendance at pre-school, incomplete education and post-schooling qualifications. The results of the study, published as a report and a book, were widely used in social policy debates in Australia concerning entrenched disadvantage, social inclusion strategies and the long-term commitment required by all government authorities to improve the life chances and experiences of many individuals and communities (Vinson, 2007).

In secondary data analysis, a form of meta-analysis can also be used to reanalyse data from several research projects that have looked at the same or very similar research questions. This approach is used by research collaborations such as the Cochrane Collaboration and Campbell Collaboration, and we discuss this in more detail in Chapter 8 when we consider the constructive appraisal of research studies.

Longitudinal studies

This is where an individual, group or community is followed over a long period of time. The best-known example in the UK is the National Child Development Study (NCDS) which has tracked more than 5000 people born in the first week of March 1946. Longitudinal studies often take place in phases, with different teams of researchers becoming involved. However, a unifying thread is the ongoing collection and interpretation of information and, usually, the location of the data in a centralized repository. Data from the NCDS, for example, are located within the Economic and Social Data Service. Although these projects are usually undertaken by large, well-resourced research teams, there is potential for smaller tracking exercises to be initiated or for follow-through to take place using previous or existing research projects.

Surveys

Surveys, used as a research approach, are undoubtedly one of the most popular ways of generating information. These can be done as a 'one-off' exercise, be repeated at agreed intervals or be carried out on a continuous basis every ten years or so, as with the UK General Household Survey. Surveys are designed to obtain data in relation to the main research question and related sub-questions, usually means of a structured questionnaire. They are also frequently used in longitudinal studies which take place over a significant period of time. Survey data are also often used to highlight areas for more intensive qualitative research.

Surveys produce descriptive statistics that can be used to identify trends. The applicability of the findings to the general population is related to the sampling method used as well as to the statistical significance of the data. Surveys can be administered by post, where the individual completes a standard questionnaire, or by means of an interview with a trained interviewer. Questionnaires usually include 'closed questions' where the participant chooses from a number of set responses, with some facility for 'open' questions, where the participant can give responses in their own words.

―――――――――――――――― **Researcher Reflection 6.1** ――――――――――――――――

Designing a quantitative project

Think about your good idea turned into a viable research question.
  How would you apply a quantitative orientation?
  Map this out.
  Reflect on this process.

MIXED METHOD APPROACHES

Mixed method approaches are those which use both quantitative and qualitative orientations. They combine the collection of quantitative factual data with a qualitatively orientated drilling-down to explore meanings, perceptions and understandings so that the research question is explored from a variety of angles.

When looking at the operation of mixed method approaches a useful example draws from the Evaluation of the Personal Health Budget Pilot Programme (Forder et al., 2012). As highlighted in Chapter 7, the methodology used to carry out an evaluation is the same as that used for researching generally, and although the purpose of an evaluation and a research project will be different, research methodology is multi-purpose, with the methodology chosen relating to what is most appropriate in the context of a particular research project or evaluation.

This evaluation was commissioned to run alongside a pilot programme including 64 sites. The aim was to identify whether personal health budgets brought about improved health and care outcomes when compared to conventional service delivery, with a linked aim of associating a positive result with the best way for personal health budgets to be implemented.

To give some background, the Personal Health Budget Programme was launched by the Department of Health in 2009 in the UK following the publication in 2008 of the Next Stage Review. The Personal Health Budget Programme incorporates three main elements. These relate to the personalization of support as a means of giving people greater control over their lives, with a concomitant move away from a 'one size fits all' culture; the provision of a personal budget to enable appropriate services and supports to be purchased; and self-directed support, which is the means by which the personal budget is estimated using the resource allocation system, a points-based formula whereby a practitioner assessor estimates a cost based on what the person might have received using traditional services or an 'off-the-shelf system' (Department of Health, 2011; Slasberg et al., 2012). Direct payments, which can be part of, but are not the same as, self-directed support, followed from the Community Care (Direct Payments) Act 1996 and the Health and Social Care Act 2001. Personalized health budgets form a key part of the personalization agenda across health care services in England. The overarching aim is to improve patient outcomes by placing patients at the centre of decisions about their care. It is related to a move to encourage a more responsive health and social care system by enabling patients to work alongside health service professionals in developing and executing a care plan utilizing a known budget. The intention is to give people greater flexibility, choice and control.

In the evaluation, quantitative and qualitative data collection points were identified to explore two key areas: patient outcome and experiences, with this including individual outcome data, primary and secondary care service use, information about care/support plans and data on patient outcomes and experiences; and implementation experiences and costs, with this including the pilot sites' experiences of implementing personal health budgets. A key aspect of the methodology incorporated the use of a controlled trial with a pragmatic design to compare the experiences of people selected to receive personal health budgets with the experiences of people continuing under existing arrangements.

The use of controlled trials as a major data collection method in health services generally has a long history. Their use in the collection of social data, as highlighted elsewhere in this book, remains controversial but is widespread. In this study a design was chosen that reflected two different configuration arrangements. The first focused on a traditional approach so that in those sites where personal health budget pilots were already operating, a health professional with responsibility for the care of individuals assessed those who were potentially eligible for a personal health budget and randomly allocated individuals into either the personal health budget group or the control group. All were asked to participate, but those in the personal health budget group were offered a budget and those in the control group continued with existing provision. The second looked to recruit participants from sites where personal health budgets were in operation (for the personal health budget group) and from similar sites where these were not (for the control group).

Quantitative and qualitative data relating to the points highlighted above were then collected over a 24-month period. With regard to the quantitative data collected on patient outcome and experiences, outcome data was collected at four key points: at the time of consent (baseline); 6 months after the date of consent, which constituted the initial follow-up; 12 months after the date of consent (the main follow-up); and up to 24 months after the date of consent (second follow-up). Data was collected by means of structured interview and postal questionnaires and covered demographic information such as age, ethnicity, sexual orientation, gender, religion, household composition and accommodation and marital status, as well as socio-demographic information associated with highest education level, type of income, current circumstances, activities of daily living, receipt of informal care support and employment status.

The postal questionnaires also focused on rating scales looking at health-related quality of life, care-related quality of life, psychological well-being, subjective well-being, perceived quality of life and perceived health. At the baseline and main follow-up stages, medical records relating to participants' health status and their use of primary and secondary health care services were also compared, together with information about secondary health care service use from hospital episode statistics.

This study was very much looking at impact and, as such, in line with other studies primarily focusing on impact, needed to draw up what is called a counterfactual. This relates to what would have happened if the particular intervention under scrutiny had not taken place – in this instance, if a personal health budget had not been allocated. The difference between what happens with intervention and what happens without is seen to be a primary measure of effectiveness. As highlighted by Forder et al. (2012), there are two key ways of measuring the difference. The first looks at before and after criteria – before the intervention and after the intervention. Although useful, from a quantitative perspective, criticism is concerned with the difficulty in ascertaining whether differences relate to the intervention or to extraneous factors. The second method is to use a randomized controlled trial – assigning individuals seen to have the same baseline credentials to two different groups, one which involves the intervention and the other which does not. As highlighted, these tests continue to be regarded as both reliable and valid provided those involved do not know if they are in the intervention or non-intervention group. The argument for this is that if individuals know which group they have been assigned to, this will change their behaviour, biasing a counterfactual.

It is notable that the feedback from the pilot sites for this study suggested that there was significant ethical concern generated about the randomized controlled trial element as this involved denying people, eligible for a personal budget, access to this way of working due to the requirements of randomization. Establishing that participants had the same baseline credentials also proved difficult. Further, local services had to collect additional data from people not benefiting from the intervention being piloted.

As a result of these concerns, in relation to other projects, Glasby (2012) has taken forward a new approach, the observational multibaseline approach. This compares outcomes before, during and after the intervention to explore impact. A key advantage is that as baseline data are collected for everyone, participants can act as their own controls. However, as this method deviates from the 'gold standard' it remains controversial.

In relation to the qualitative information obtained for the study, semi-structured interviews were used with a subsample of personal health budget holders 3 months after the giving of consent, with a follow-up at the 9-month stage. These attempted to recruit a cross-section of personal health budget holders and at 3 months focused on how people found out about personal health budgets, together with their initial impressions, their knowledge of the amount of the budget and how this had been calculated, their decisions about how to use the budget and the help received with this, and the options for managing the budget. At the 9-month stage, emphasis was placed on the perceived impacts of the personal health budget on budget holders' health, well-being and quality of life; reflections on their chosen use of the budget; satisfaction with the amount of the budget; reflections on the way the budget had been managed; and experiences of the implementation of the personal health budget.

With regard to implementation experiences and costs, again both quantitative and qualitative data collection techniques were used to explore pilot sites' experiences of how the personal health budgets had been implemented. The quantitative data collection exercise was orientated around key frontline operational staff completing a web-based questionnaire after 3 and 24 months. This looked at the extent to which the implementation of personal health budgets had an impact on the workplace environment, with associated measures such as job satisfaction or lack of it and occupational stress also featuring. Information about the costs associated with implementing personal health budgets during the first and second year of the local pilot programmes was also collected by means of a template at 12 months and 24 months.

The qualitative emphasis was associated with interviewing a variety of operational staff, frontline professionals, third-party budget holders and commissioning managers at the 3-month, 15-month and 24-month stages. Information was collected here on the challenges and barriers encountered, how these were addressed, as well as the impact of personal health budgets on the wider local health and social care economy and patterns of service provision.

It is notable that for the quantitative data analysis, a power calculation was required to assess the viability of the sample size for obtaining statistically significant results.

For this study it was estimated that 1000 participants needed to be recruited to both the personal health budget and the control groups.

In this study, the quantitative data analysis focused on a 'difference-in-difference' approach. This recognizes that intervention and control groups can differ at the baseline stage, and that during the course of the intervention other factors could exert influence. In this study, instead of comparing the post-intervention outcome indicators between groups, they compared the changes in the outcome indicator between baseline and follow-up for the two groups. They measured effectiveness by subtracting the follow-up score minus the baseline in the outcome indicator for the control group from the same change in the outcome indicator for the intervention group. This was based on the assumption that without the intervention, the situation relating to the intervention group would show an average change that equated to that of the control group. They therefore designated the counterfactual to be the change in the outcome indicator between the groups.

The analysis was designed, by the use of the difference-in-difference approach, to remove the differences between the groups in the level of the outcome indicator at baseline. Forder et al. (2012) acknowledged that whilst this method is an effective way to control for differences in the characteristics, there is a possibility that differences between the groups might cause differences in the rate of change of the indicator, distorting the findings. They tried to rectify this by using multi-variate difference-in difference models, which, they maintained, allowed them to identify and remove the effects of differences in baseline characteristics between the groups on change in the outcome measures.

The outcome indicators used reflected the rating scale areas (clinical outcomes, health-related quality of life, care-related quality of life, subjective well-being, perceived quality of life, perceived health, with the addition of mortality). This was then measured using the difference-in-difference method, with each aspect of each rating scale being given a weighting largely using population-based preferences. For example, a weighting for control over daily life would be given as: desired, 5.18; adequate, 1.5; and poor, 0. Relating this to the relevant rating scale, the option 'I have as much control over my daily life as I want' would be ascribed a 'no' need level, 'Sometimes I don't feel I have as much control over my daily life' a 'low' need level, and 'I have no control over my daily life' a 'high' need level. If a person reported that their level of control was at a desired level, this would be scored at 5.18.

The qualitative data were analysed using a form of thematic analysis called the framework approach (Ritchie and Spencer, 1994). This involved the data being summarized and quotations extracted from each transcript. These summaries were then placed in a template organized by themes, with the themes being based on the topics included in the interview topic guides. By means of the template, the themes were compared in relation to participants and personal budget holder and control groupings.

Although the findings of this study, used as an illustrative case study of the use of mixed methods in this chapter, are not directly relevant, given the emphasis on methodology, it is still useful and informative to report that the use of personal health budgets was associated with a significant improvement in care-related quality of life as well as psychological well-being. However, no other significant differences were found with regard to the other indicators used.

Mixed methods can generally be seen as an effective means of combining wide-ranging factual information with a concomitant drilling-down to make sense of the information collected. This facilitates an exploration of understandings and meanings and allows for interpretative analysis. However, Bryman (2008) in 'Reflections on mixed method research' highlights the need for rigour, for the method chosen to be applicable to the research question, for attention to be paid to not diluting the research effort by spreading resources too thinly, and the importance of spending time on the integration of the findings. Nevertheless, mixed method research can be seen to be both increasing in popularity and becoming 'par for the course' for larger research projects.

CONCLUDING REMARKS

In this chapter the utility of quantitative orientations has been reviewed and examples given of how these can be effectively employed to take forward the research project following on from the formulation of the key research question based on the good idea. Controversy persists between proponents of qualitative and quantitative orientations, with the former questioning the extent to which statistical provenance can be given to measures of reliability, validity and generalizability in the social field. They also give voice to ethical concerns and, in particular, to participants continuing to be researched 'on' rather than 'with'. The latter group, in turn, continue to raise questions of bias and methodological soundness. However, it can be asserted that for both, provided the researcher in their translation of their good idea into a viable research project pays attention to ontological and epistemological issues, to ethical sensitivity and to methodological appropriateness, both rigour and matters of participation can be adhered to.

Mixed method research is a means of combining quantitative and qualitative methodologies in order to obtain information about what is going on in relation to a particular area and to drill down to the formative interpretations. This is a way of researching which emphasizes commonalities between research orientations rather than differences and can be seen, perhaps a little paradoxically, to be breaking down the traditional divide between quantitative and qualitative approaches. In the next chapter we will look at evaluative researching and consider the benefits and also the pitfalls of this form of research.

SEVEN

Evaluative researching

While similar methodologies are used for evaluative researching as for other forms of research, 'evaluation' is often seen to lack the status of other forms of research. This chapter will review definitions of evaluation and the various ways in which evaluative research can be carried out. The chapter promotes evaluation as a key method of research, and its place as a legitimate research approach is discussed. Inclusive and emancipatory approaches will be considered in designing research and in the interpretation of findings.

Researchers and potential researchers usually begin with abstract ideas or phenomena that they are interested in knowing more about. These ideas or concepts are operationalized in particular ways depending on the research tradition involved. In the case of quantitative studies, dependent and independent variables are identified in a hypothetical relationship that is investigated with the aim of proving causal relationships between them. In qualitative studies, phenomena and concepts are explored thematically within theoretical and contextual frameworks that seek to find deeper understanding and meaning of the experiences and realities of participants in particular situations. In evaluative researching, the programme or activity to be evaluated establishes the parameters of the research task. However, as we explore this type of researching, we will see these relationships may be approached in different ways depending on a number of factors. In our exploration of evaluative researching we will look more closely at the ways in which it can be understood and positioned with equal status to other approaches within specific research contexts. Evaluative researching uses quantitative and qualitative methods and the ways in which these can be utilized will be discussed with the aim of revitalizing the merits of evaluative researching as a legitimate approach.

EXPLORING EVALUATIVE RESEARCH

In thinking about what it means to evaluate something, we usually think of 'weighing up', appraising the value of something, estimating the worth of a particular course of action, forming an opinion and, most importantly, making a judgement about the worth of an action. Once these processes have been completed, they are usually followed by decisions regarding the continuation, modification or cessation of what is being evaluated. Continuing an action may involve making no changes at all (continuing 'as is') or making changes that add to the value or worth of the action (continuing 'with modifications'). If the value or worth of an action is deemed to be negligible or not meeting its purpose, then ceasing the action may be an outcome. In this chapter we use one approach to evaluative research, that of programme evaluation, as the platform to discuss this type of research. This approach begins with the programme or activity to be evaluated. In doing so the discussion is underpinned with themes of inclusion and participation. Other approaches to evaluative research, sometimes referred to as participatory evaluation, begin with people's experiences as participants in or with the activity being evaluated. This measures the significance of a social programme through the lives of those engaged with it (Stake, 1967; Kushner, 2000).

In using some of these everyday terms, such as 'value', 'worth', 'weighing up', 'estimation', 'judgement' and 'decision', it is clear that research activities that draw from understandings of evaluation will include some quite different features compared to other research approaches. White (2010: 379) suggests that evaluative research is inherently 'political' as it is 'ultimately about making judgments, that in turn have consequences for the "actors" or those involved in the evaluation'. Interpretation of and influence on the dimensions of all the elements involved in this type of research mean that evaluative researching is more 'overtly politicized than other types of social research' (p. 379). These elements of evaluative researching can make it vulnerable to claims of manipulation and 'unscientific' approaches. More so than other types of social research, evaluative research has been used in the past to modify and close down programmes that have not been viewed as meeting prevailing understandings of worthiness or effectiveness but which may, when assessed against other criteria, be regarded as highly successful and worthwhile.

There are a number of approaches to evaluative research. The most common of these takes the form of a research inquiry about an existing programme or activity. Two further unique features of this approach to evaluative researching are the research imperative, or the way it usually comes about, and the relationship of the staff working in the programme or activity with those undertaking the evaluation. Sometimes they can be the same – staff working on a programme may either undertake the research themselves or request that other researchers undertake it on their behalf. Alternatively, they may be research participants or subjects where the research is auspiced and undertaken by others external to the programme. Examples of external groups are funding bodies, administrators, government agencies and professional associations.

Evaluative researching has its historical base in the emergence of programmes and activities set up to meet particular societal needs. It thus has strong connections with understandings of social policy or the way in which groups interact and form relationships in society. In the 1970s and 1980s a growing body of literature contextualized evaluative research as primarily programme evaluation, with authors such as Suchman (1967: 7) defining evaluative research as 'the utilization of scientific research methods for the purpose of making an evaluation (a judgment of worth)' and Rossi and Freeman (1982: 20) defining evaluative research as 'the systematic application of social research procedures in assessing the conceptualization and design, implementation and utility of social intervention programs'. In these developing definitions of evaluation some key elements were beginning to emerge. These were the identified needs that the programme aimed to meet, the implementation processes undertaken within it and the final outcomes of the activity.

In underscoring the political dimension of evaluative research, Posavac and Carey (1980: 6) defined programme evaluation as 'a collection of methods, skills and sensitivities necessary to determine whether a human service is needed and likely to be used, whether it is conducted as planned, and whether the human service actually does help people in need'. We will look more closely at this dimension in the later section on evaluative research and policy practices.

Researcher Reflection 7.1

Evaluative research in the workplace

In your workplace can you identify a programme that has recently been evaluated?

Who initiated the evaluation?

Who completed the evaluation?

What were the stated objectives of the evaluation?

What methods were used?

What was the outcome?

How were the results disseminated?

Can you identify any 'political' imperatives?

SHAPING UNDERSTANDINGS OF 'NEEDS' AND ISSUES OF CONCERN

In understanding evaluative researching, it is important first to understand how the programmes and activities that are the focus for evaluation have come about. Once we understand this we are then more able to answer the key question in evaluative research: whether the programme achieved the identified purpose for which it was established. A programme's purpose can be more deeply understood if we consider it as a way of meeting particular needs in society and ask why it was set up. Community workers, social scientists and others use needs assessments as a tool of practice to build a picture of situations. They may be undertaken as part of broader societal initiatives that aim to intervene in, solve, manage or control particular societal phenomena. Similarly, evaluative researchers draw on this approach in understanding the reasons why a programme or activity was undertaken. A needs analysis or assessment draws from a range of source material that can be prospective and/or retrospective in nature. It can include primary source data collected by the researcher, or secondary source data including existing data sets, literature reviews and previous studies from which a need may be determined.

Drilling down, further needs can be categorized according to certain attributes (Bradshaw, 1977). Needs can be 'normative', where the provision of a particular service or action establishes a desirable standard for recipients. For example, a government programme may roll out the provision of laptop computers or other personal IT devices to all school students to support student education. In the case of normative needs, however, what constitutes the 'desirable' standard is contingent on the particular lens through which the standard has been created. In what specific ways will educational support be realized through this desirable standard? Will all students have equal access to the same IT resources?

'Felt' or perceived needs are those determined by the individual about their own particular circumstances in relation to their community and environment. For example, young people in rural areas with poor internet access may feel isolated without devices that support their connection to social media.

'Expressed needs' are those needs that have become articulated and formulated into specific demands and expectations. So, in the same example, communities with poor internet access may express their need to take advantage of the roll-out and meet what others consider to be a normative need by advocating with local school authorities and decision-makers for improved services.

Advocating is a social work term. A more generic term might be 'making representations to' or 'lobbying'. The sentence could also continue '… by advocating with local school authorities and decision-makers for improved services.

Finally, needs can be understood as 'relative' or 'comparative', where they illustrate gaps of provision between groups in the community or between communities. For example, schools in areas of socio-economic disadvantage may receive priority over others in identifying and meeting such needs.

A more critical analysis of needs, however, demonstrates that the concept of 'need' and its various iterations facilitate the structure of provision within the values, beliefs and dominant world-views of groups and communities at a particular point in time. In a socialist-feminist critique of needs, Fraser (1990: 199) opens her argument with a quotation from Foucault: 'Need is also a political instrument, meticulously prepared, calculated and used' (Foucault, 1977: 26). She argues that 'needs-talk is a medium for the making and contesting of political claims ... where inequalities are symbolically elaborated and challenged' (Fraser, 1990: 199), thus positioning power and privileged discourses as the means by which needs are understood. Further critical analysis might lead researchers to consider the potentially competitive positions of 'needs' versus 'rights' discourses, being mindful of the previously discussed critique of rights-based work espoused by Ife (2008), discussed in Chapter 3. As a reminder, Ife argues that the rights discourse has created a dichotomy between 'the powerful' and 'the powerless' which continues to objectify those it aims to liberate. It might be argued that the 'needs' discourse similarly objectifies those it aims to assist, sustaining 'programme recipients' as powerless rather than as equal participants, co-producers or autonomous programme directors. In considering needs through the lens of inequalities and inequities we begin to shift understandings of physical and social differences (inequalities) and the unequal distribution of power and resources (inequities) in and between groups and communities. We argue that evaluative researchers need to understand and critically review the conceptualization of 'needs' and the criteria against which programmes and activities are evaluated to ensure inclusive, participatory and emancipatory approaches. In the remainder of this chapter, instead of using the term 'need' we will use 'issue of concern' to identify the reasons for which a programme or activity has been established. The analysis of needs, rights or inequities is determined by theoretical positioning and is usually the starting point in determining what type of programme or activity should be established to alleviate the circumstances that have been identified.

If we turn now to the components of evaluative researching in more detail, the first step is identifying and scoping the issue of concern for which the programme was developed. This is interrogated through a series of questions that establish the parameters of the issue of concern and is often referred to as scoping work. Kettner et al. (1990) and White (2010) list similar components of the scoping exercise:

- What is the nature of the issue of concern, problem, situation or condition that the programme or activity has been aiming to address?
- What terms and ideas are being used and how are they defined and understood?
- Who is experiencing the issue of concern or situation and what is the extent of this experience?
- Are there statistical or other data available illustrating the dimensions of the issue or situation, including incidence and prevalence?
- Are there interest groups or stakeholders and how do they perceive the situation? (Compare these questions to those identified in Chapter 2.)
- Under what circumstances has the issue or situation come about?
- What are the circumstances of the evaluation, i.e. why is it being undertaken and by whom?

In the context of contemporary discussions regarding the available 'evidence' for certain types of interventions or actions, a further question may be:

- What is already known about the issue or concern that has been expressed as research 'evidence' for actions or ways of intervening?

EVALUATIVE RESEARCH AND INCLUSION

The scoping exercise begins with a statement of the issue of concern that, on closer critical examination, will reflect the ways in which a programme or activity is designed and subsequently evaluated using indicators of performance that measure and assess the achievement of outcomes. This in turn reflects the positioning or relationship with knowledge of the programme designers.

In this chapter we have developed examples from the education field for some of the researcher reflections. For a wider discussion of research methods in education research, including evaluative studies, see Green et al. (2006).

Researcher Reflection 7.2

Developing an evaluation study

An inner-city junior school has enrolled a large number of students from refugee families who have recently moved into the community. Of the 500 students at the school, nearly a third are children from families where English is not spoken at home. Teachers at the school have requested a meeting with the school principal about this situation.

What is/are the issue/s of concern in this situation?

Select one issue of concern that you have formulated and develop a brief scoping statement for each of the suggested components.

Briefly outline one or two programmes that might be undertaken in response to the formulated issue of concern.

Many responses will undoubtedly state the issue of concern as being the inability of newly enrolled students to speak English proficiently. An aim or objective of programmes that might be set up in response to this issue may be focused on improving English language proficiency by putting in place particular activities. Whilst teaching English to speakers of other languages may be an overarching objective, the way in which this is undertaken may reflect the values, priorities and resources of key stakeholders in the situation, including the teachers, the school board and governing body, funding authorities, parent associations, school teachers, school students, their families and the local community.

The development of the programme or activities will reflect the understanding of the issue of concern determined by these factors.

Let us now look in more detail at some possible programmes that might be developed to improve the English language skills of recently enrolled children. One possible programme may provide voluntary English language classes after school, and another may be to integrate English language education into the existing lesson plans of the curriculum. Both of these actions can be set up as programmes to be evaluated which would draw on the technical understandings of evaluative researching. The aims of each of these programmes are underpinned by the belief that English proficiency will be of benefit to the children. Views about the stated issue of concern that demonstrate inclusivity may be based on beliefs that a sense of belonging and social connectedness are valued and that a way to achieve this is through English language proficiency. Inclusive approaches that involve the joint development of programmes with the refugee parents and children themselves are underpinned by further considerations and actions that incorporate, integrate and include differing ways of knowing and learning about language. Emancipatory approaches may extend this further to an engagement with the local community where educational approaches are developed together with parents and children in participatory relationships with school teachers and other stakeholders.

Returning to Researcher Reflection 7.2 and the programmes you briefly outlined, consider these further questions:

Researcher Reflection 7.3

Further issues to consider – silent voices

In the programmes you outlined, which stakeholders are prominent? Whose voices are silent?

In what ways are the suggested responses inclusive of the refugee families and their children?

Whichever programme is established, it will be evaluated drawing on understood evaluative methods. However, it is important to remember that in evaluative researching the formulation of the criteria (sometimes called performance indicators) by which a programme, action or intervention is evaluated can also include criteria about inclusivity. Hence a desired outcome of the programme, rather than being to teach the asylum seeker students English, may be to support the active engagement and participation of the refugee families in the life of the school, and one of the measurement criteria of this outcome may be the English language proficiency of the students.

In considering these possible programmes, reviewing available research on the issue would also be an important step in the scoping process.

──────────────── **Researcher Reflection 7.4** ────────────────

Finding available evidence

What does the available evidence from previous research tell us about this issue?

A keyword search of the Campbell Collaboration database of systematic reviews found the following review: 'Impacts of After-School Programs on Student Outcomes: A Systematic Review' (Zief et al., 2006). The review applied rigorous inclusion and exclusion criteria and analysed the findings of included studies. The findings were not conclusive and stated in part:

> While this review has included the most rigorous studies conducted of after-school programs that are currently of great policy interest due to their inclusion of academic support components, reviewers note that the collected evidence is not sufficient to make any policy or programming recommendations. While some areas of promise do exist – supervision and participation in activities – these pooled impacts need to be tested with further research. (p. 25)

The Campbell Collaboration review can be found at: http://campbellcollaboration.org/lib/project/12

However, although inconclusive, the studies provide useful information for those wishing to set up a similar programme and evaluate its effectiveness. Some social researchers, such as Yegidis and Weinbach (2008) and Dodd and Epstein (2012), would argue that although in empirical terms the statistical significance is questionable, the *social* significance and value of the studies is still evident. A fuller discussion of the constructive appraisal of research and the use of research evidence is included in Chapter 8.

EVALUATIVE RESEARCH AND TRUSTWORTHINESS

When undertaking evaluative research, once an issue of concern or a situation is understood the researcher may then begin to consider the hypothesis that underpins the programme or activity. Whilst this term comes from quantitative researching, it can still be a useful means of understanding the purpose of programmes and activities. This purpose may not always be explicit, but should be articulated by the researcher in examining the scoping process. The research questions developed by the evaluative researcher are then formulated around the effectiveness of the programme or activity to achieve the stated purpose.

Put simply, a programme hypothesis is based on the relationship between the actions involved in the programme and the desired outcome: in doing x in a particular way $x + 1$, then y will result which will lead to z being achieved. These are sometimes called inputs, throughputs, outputs and outcomes.

--- **Researcher Reflection 7.5** ---

Identifying the programme hypothesis

Returning to the school example again, consider the programmes that you developed or the examples provided and identify the programme hypothesis in each.

What actions or activities are involved?

How will they be undertaken? Where and by whom?

What are the indicators of achievement? (For example, students' weekly test results may show improvement by 10% in spelling, comprehension and conversational English.)

What are the desired outcomes? (For example, after completing the programme students will be able to participate in classroom discussion in English and will be able to complete a set piece of work in English.)

Evaluative research methods usually involve three types of research design. *Experimental and quasi-experimental designs* involve the measurement of the effect of a particular activity. For a more comprehensive explanation of the method, see Campbell et al. (1963). The simplest type of design is the 'pre-experimental' study, sometimes referred to as the 'one-shot case study', that provides some immediate information for a particular purpose. This approach involves the articulation of a programme outcome to be achieved – the development of criteria for measurement that in turn leads to a statement about the success of the programme. In the example of teaching students English, an after-school English language class may run during term one afternoon per week. The criteria for the success of the programme may be the teacher-reported improvement in English comprehension in regular classes during the term. This approach may include a further comparative factor such as a 'pre and post' activity where testing English proficiency occurs before and after the programme to demonstrate a change in the student participants. A further design feature may include the introduction of a time factor to explain differences; so testing may occur at various times during the school term, for example at the beginning of the term, before and after the mid-term break and at the end of term. The results would then be compared. Experimental design introduces more systematic sampling and randomization of participants in the evaluation. In the school example, students may be randomly allocated to two after-school classes and the outcomes measured. This approach draws on established quantitative research methods that aim to establish a causal effect of a particular intervention, in this case the teaching of English in an after-school group that results in the improvement of English proficiency. This may be studied over a period of time, for example repeating the evaluation each year and comparing the results.

Each research tradition, whether it be quantitative or qualitative, has strengths and limitations that must be taken into account when interpreting results. In the case of experimental and quasi-experimental designs in evaluative researching where 'pre' and 'post' situations are evaluated, the constantly changing conditions in which the situations exist mean that researchers cannot control the variables as they may do in other types of quantitative researching. This is sometimes referred to as 'point in time' data. In the case of the school students learning English, other factors such as their exposure to public and social media in daily life may have facilitated language proficiency. This could not be a controlled variable in the experimental studies. Qualitative methods such as in-depth interviews and observation would complement the pre- and post-testing methods to enable a better sense of developmental learning, reflecting a mixed methods approach.

The other two design methods in evaluative researching are drawn from qualitative research paradigms. Sometimes referred to as *naturalistic designs* (as opposed to quantitative designs), they aim to evaluate the effectiveness of a particular programme or activity within the reality and experience of those involved. These designs may use qualitative methods such as in-depth interviews, observation, engagement with the local environment, thick description of events, and the review of different sources of material such as formal and informal written material. In the case of the school study, an evaluative researcher may send out an invitation to the refugee parents, translated into the language spoken at home, to participate in an interview about the English language classes. The researcher may also interview teachers and other stakeholders and review documents about the programme both within the school and perhaps outside the school such as via the local media or other sources. They may also attend and observe classes and may undertake a literature review, reading widely about the situation.

Another method involves the evaluation of decisions and processes leading to the establishment and running of a programme. Sometimes referred to as *contextual analysis*, it tends to focus on the outputs or processes surrounding the implementation of a particular programme. In this approach, the reasons for setting up and running the programme in a particular way are investigated. In the case of the school study, an evaluative study may include the researcher examining formal and informal documentation about the programme; how the need was identified and the types of inputs that were made to the programme (for example, whether sufficient funds were made available); how teachers were selected for the programme (for example, whether they were trained in teaching English to speakers of other languages); and how cultural competencies were incorporated into lesson plans.

Researchers using evaluative methods need to be mindful of the strengths and limitations of each design method. A key strength of quantitative methods in evaluative researching is that they can quickly demonstrate the effect of a particular action or intervention, justifying a programme's utility and sustainability. This is particularly useful for submissions for ongoing funding. A key strength of naturalistic understandings of programmes and their effectiveness in meeting particular situations, problems or concerns is that they can make significant contributions to the wider cultural, contextual and political environment in which programmes operate.

—————————— **Researcher Reflection 7.6** ——————————

Programme hypotheses and outcomes from different perspectives

A community centre, which is adjacent to a large residential estate, wishes to set aside an area in the grounds of the centre for a newly funded programme. The new programme, 'Exercise for Health and Fun', is for older residents. The centre plans to install fixed exercise equipment that the manufacturer has advised will be suitable for older users.

Imagine you are the funding body and consider your answers to the following questions:

What is the programme hypothesis?

What type of evidence will you require to demonstrate the programme's effectiveness?

What are the desirable programme outcomes that will lead to the continuation of funding for the programme?

Imagine you are a community researcher employed by the centre to evaluate the programme and consider your answers to the following questions:

What is the programme hypothesis?

What indicators could be developed and measured to demonstrate inclusivity in the programme? For example, to what extent do local older residents participate in decision-making about the exercise programme?

What outcomes can be identified, measured and evaluated, drawing on inclusive practices?

In what ways do these approaches reflect different approaches to evaluative researching?

EVALUATIVE RESEARCH AND POLICY PRACTICES

A more recent trend in evaluative researching is the assessment of the impact of particular actions and activities. Since the mid-1990s the emergence of *impact statements* can be seen as a feature of policy and planning. Originating from the green movement, the most commonly recognized statements are environmental impact statements. These are now commonly embedded in legislation and are required by planning authorities in most jurisdictions in development applications in the built environment. Consideration of the impact of proposals includes statements about natural and social ecosystems (habitat and protected flora and fauna); the impact on architectural, anthropological, historical, cultural and local communities; risks and safety concerns; pollution and waste disposal; integration with the current environment; and the impact on general amenities.

As understandings of the interdependence of the physical and social environment have developed, increasing emphasis has been placed on social elements that contribute to population health and quality of life. In the last two decades these impacts have been expressed in new types of evaluative statements known as health impact assessments (HIAs). Here the term 'health' is conceptualized broadly to include social, economic, environmental and physical elements. These statements reflect different historical, interdisciplinary and epistemological views emerging from three fields: environmental health; social views of health; and health equity (Harris-Roxas and Harris, 2011). Significantly, HIAs are used by organizations such as the World Health Organization, the UK National Health Service and the national and state governments of many countries in the formulation and implementation of policies and programmes that will have desired consequences on the improvement of health and well-being (Krieger et al., 2003). The assessment methods draw on both quantitative and qualitative research traditions, and the potential for mixed method and interdisciplinary working in the development and utilization of HIAs drawing on participatory and inclusive approaches can make a significant contribution in the policy arena.

HIAs can be critically reviewed through the same lens as other types of evaluative researching, and in such an assessment Krieger et al. identified a number of considerations related to policy and research approaches. In research approaches, in particular, links to evaluative researching are made including the need for clear theoretical frameworks, the selection of appropriate research methodology without privileging one tradition over the other, and consideration by researchers of the potential for statements to improve circumstances and/or perpetuate policies that may have overall negative consequences. It is this point in particular that has resonance for inclusive and emancipatory approaches. In a word of caution, Krieger et al. comment that the pursuit of 'evidence-based policy' to the exclusion of other approaches can be detrimental to the development of policies and programmes that have more inclusive and socially desirable outcomes. Authors such as Love et al. (2005) discuss this further, arguing that a 'negotiated relationship' between quantitative and qualitative approaches (which are of equal value and significance) should be undertaken to ensure that optimal policy outcomes are achieved.

In reviewing the typologies of HIAs, Harris-Roxas and Harris (2011) have identified four domains: mandated HIAs that fulfil statutory and regulated requirements;

decision-support HIAs that are undertaken to assist and support policy and programmatic decision-making; advocacy HIAs that are used to support arguments and policy positions that may challenge existing ones; and community-led HIAs in which communities conduct the assessments themselves, thus becoming part of the policy-making process. These types of assessment often reflect participatory action research approaches. Community participation as an inclusive and emancipatory strategy involves the equal consideration of the views of stakeholders and clear decision-making processes in which community members actively participate. Posing challenges similar to other inclusive researching approaches, evaluative researchers need to be mindful of fundamental elements including comprehensive scoping activities, a shared, agreed understanding of the purpose of the evaluation, and the processes and methods to be used.

One other consideration in evaluative researching is the potential cost of undertaking projects. Whilst some evaluations are undertaken 'in house' and costs can be absorbed by the organizations and groups auspicing the work, external evaluations can be expensive and hence research grants are often a source of funding. In the case of community-led evaluations, the costs of undertaking the activities and the pursuit of funding introduces other stakeholders that in turn may influence the research scope and design. One way forward is the repositioning of evaluative researching approaches in partnership with mainstream research traditions, thus reducing the potential impact of poor policy practices being continued by inappropriate, narrow or exclusive epistemological considerations.

In the earlier part of this chapter we briefly mentioned the connections between the development of programmes as a feature of social and public policy responses and the consequent evaluation of these programmes as a research approach. Programme evaluation is a research method that aims to determine the value, worth and effectiveness of programmes against formulated criteria. These activities occur within contexts that need to be understood by the researcher and those who may use the research to justify particular actions that may follow. We have also referred to the ways in which values, knowledge and political imperatives can influence why the evaluation is occurring, who is conducting it, what is evaluated and how it is to be conducted. These world-views can be instrumental in the programmatic policy response and subsequent evaluation.

In the late 1980s and 1990s the elements of evaluation and evaluative methods were largely seen as a tool of managerialism and the approach began to take on the language of the market, reflecting the dominant neoliberal discourse of this period (Ife, 1997; Prasad, 2006: Payne, 2012). Programme evaluation as a research approach was seen as a research tool that could be understood exclusively in scientifically orientated positivist terms measuring and monitoring the performance of programmes. In the human services sector programmes were evaluated according to their impact and utility against desirable goals. This approach was dominated by the prevailing values of cost-effectiveness relative to outcome or 'result'. At the height of neoliberalism in the last two decades of the twentieth century, some elements of evaluative researching were generalized to an operational level within organizations including those in the human services sector. This included the development of corporate values, mission statements, performance indicators, efficiency auditing, management review, risk management, quality assurance and programme evaluation, all of which aimed to measure the impact, outputs and outcomes of organizations against objective criteria. Poorly designed evaluative practices often resulted in programmes being closed down or significantly cut back, thus demonstrating the 'political' nature of this type of research. Those approaches that adapted, modified and reduced features of evaluative researching for different purposes had the effect of diminishing the value of evaluative researching and its trustworthiness as a legitimate research method.

Reclaiming the method as a research activity, White (2010) identifies a number of underpinning features including reflection; organizational, cultural and social contexts; moral and ethical responsibilities in relation to conducting the research and possible outcomes; and the need for constant review. These features should be present in evaluative researching whether quantitative and/or qualitative methods are being used. Their presence in evaluative researching enhances opportunities for inclusive, participatory and emancipatory approaches to be incorporated into evaluative research design. The potential influence on policy practices of the outcomes of evaluation can be seen in the recommendations that arise from evaluative researching.

An example of this is a study by Rawsthorne and Hoffman (2010) where the evaluation resulted in recommendations that had important policy imperatives. The study evaluated a peer education programme for young women that was part of a violence prevention initiative developed by a local women's health centre. The early intervention programme aimed to facilitate young women's understandings of healthy, non-violent intimate relationships and, in so doing, support the young women to form such relationships in their own lives. The externally funded programme was run in eight local schools over a three-year period and involved young women aged 14–15 years. The theoretical underpinnings of the programme were based on feminist understandings of violence that included gender roles and power imbalances, cultural perspectives and social roles and expectations. The school-based programme was evaluated using self-administered pre- and post-questionnaires completed by young women participating in the programme. The questionnaires included a case scenario with open-ended questions that were qualitatively analysed. Whilst the programme evaluation resulted in several positive outcomes, including an increased awareness of what constituted abusive relationships, the 'point in time' results were further supported by a comprehensive discussion of the study as a policy initiative in the research report for the funding body and the subsequent publication in a peer-reviewed journal. Implications for policy development that focused on prevention of violence against women included recommendations for a 'multi-pronged and multi-level strategy' that involved peer education not only for young women but also for young men, specific policy initiatives in school practices, gendered 'household' practices and the 'normalization' of the need for non-violent relationships amongst groups that have been historically vulnerable, such as adolescent girls and young women.

CONCLUDING REMARKS

Our starting point in this chapter was to explore the elements of evaluative researching with a view to repositioning it as a method of equivalent status with other approaches. Understanding these differences and using them to advantage can support research initiatives that can be effective, inclusive and participatory. In other types of research the researcher may have more autonomy in determining the research question, the data to work with, the method to be used and the epistemological lens through which the findings will be interpreted and understood. Although these elements may already be established to a greater degree in evaluative research, in reclaiming the method and privileging the underpinning features, evaluative researching can resume its place and status as a key research method. Drawing on more sophisticated awareness of multiple knowledge frames and experienced realities, the evaluative researcher can incorporate features that support and facilitate quantitative and qualitative approaches. Evaluation studies that draw on these elements can lead to the continuation of programmes that have been evaluated as effective and that have emancipatory outcomes. Approaches to evaluative research can also be 'turned around', beginning not with the programme or activity to be evaluated, but with people's experiences and the impact on their lives as a way of measuring and understanding it. The evaluation and design of programmes and activities in these ways will lead on to the identification of new research agendas and the formulation of policy practices that are more responsive to issues of concern.

EIGHT

Constructively and critically appraising research

This chapter discusses how to read research, how to take account of language and context and how to ascertain rigour and relevance. We will pay attention to how the context of the writing determines what is included and how it needs to be interpreted. This involves the researcher locating themselves as a critical reader and ascertaining the links made between purpose, analysis, findings and action. This critical interrogation will be accompanied by a review of commonly used ways of producing research reports, and this chapter will draw from relevant international examples to produce signposts and markers.

In this chapter we also look at evidence-based practice and the ways in which this broad concept has been put forward as the panacea for all problems experienced in social work and health services. Accordingly, we look at different conceptualizations of what constitutes evidence, the various types of evidence, its relationship with research, research rigour in relation to evidence, and overall the utility of evidence in the arena of health and social work. As part of this process, we use examples of the relationships between evidence and practice drawn from a variety of international contexts and explore rationales, theoretical underpinning and utility.

LOOKING FOR INCLUSION

In thinking about inclusion as a desirable feature of the research endeavour, two aspects will be considered: inclusion as a feature of research orientations; and inclusion as a feature of research design and method.

Looking firstly at inclusion as a feature of research orientations, we immediately think of the dichotomies that exist between scientifically and positivistically orientated and naturalistic paradigms. It is very easy for research studies to be simplistically allocated to one of these paradigms, creating a dichotomous positioning of each, and from which each appraises the other.

The research domain is not the only area in which this type of dualism creates divisions that seemingly cannot be bridged. Other examples are the theory and practice divide; research and practice dichotomies; and 'town versus gown' or agency versus academy debates. All of these are evident in the health and social care field. The latter two, in particular, have provided fertile ground for the development of practice-based research that has emerged as a response from practitioners seeking research relevance. The crisis of confidence in professional practice based on technical rationality identified by Schön (1983) was an indicator of the beginnings of post-positivist stances where the technical basis of foundational knowledge and expertise was challenged. The super-complexity of the postmodern era (Barnett, 2007; McCune and Entwistle, 2011) has demanded different and more inclusive understandings of multiple perspectives, approaches and meanings that are given equal recognition, status and privilege.

In visioning an inclusive research environment, Plath (2006) and Epstein (2012) have suggested that all forms of research, including evidence-based practice, research-based practice and practice-based research, need to be complementary rather than conflicting alternatives. Suggesting an evidence-informed practice approach, inclusivity would be achieved through methodological pluralism that takes into account both research-based knowledge and practice wisdom. Partnerships between academic and practitioner researchers would pursue collaborative research relationships that would privilege both research-driven practice and practice-driven research. These relationships between 'co-creators' of knowledge would be both empowering and emancipatory. This knowledge would be the result of a range of methods and approaches appropriately used to seek new understandings and meanings and new information exchange. In the words of Epstein (2012), this would include 'statistical analyses of quantitative information, narratives and thematic analyses of qualitative information, technologically sophisticated and profoundly simple ways of communicating information, metaphors, stories, anecdotes, artistic expression, poetry and humour'. This approach expresses a different 'way of knowing' built on the foundation stones of research methodology, but with a resonance for the complexities of both the postmodern world and the ambiguities and complexities of the practice environment.

The impetus to pursue inclusion as a feature of research paradigms can be attributed to a number of motivations. These include securing improved accountability for research and practice claims; ensuring methodological fairness with a just approach to knowledge creation; providing opportunities for all professions to participate in research as equal stakeholders; and encouraging more critically reflective practitioners and researchers.

In a similar way, the impetus to pursue inclusion as a feature of research design and method can be attributed to these motivations with an emphasis on inclusive and equal participation by all those involved in the research activity;

on researching ethically, taking into account the moral underpinnings of the research endeavour; and on encouraging reflexivity in researchers. This has been discussed in previous chapters relating to specific research methodology.

CONSIDERING DEBATES OF TRUSTWORTHINESS

No matter what type of research is being proposed, the credibility and integrity of the research endeavour is juxtaposed with relationships of trust between the researcher, those participating in the research and the nature and purpose of the inquiry. To return to a discussion of trustworthiness, touched on in Chapter 3, irrespective of the research orientation, trustworthiness can be seen to be a belief in the moral integrity of both the researcher and the research inquiry, once again linking the research endeavour to ethical and moral decision-making.

This foundational aspect is supported by a number of other aspects, including the quality of the research; the achievement of the stated aims and objectives; and the contribution made to knowledge building.

However, researchers must also be aware of a more technical understanding of the term. In early literature on the theorization of qualitative research, the concept of 'trustworthiness' was developed to enable a means of expressing and determining those elements that had equivalence to existing understandings of reliability and validity, used as measures in quantitative methods. Models to ensure the trustworthiness of qualitative studies have been developed by Guba (1981), Lincoln and Guba (1985) and Krefting (1991). Guba's model, for example, is based on four principles: truth value, applicability, consistency and neutrality. In brief, truth value is a measure of the degree of confidence in the truth of the findings; applicability is the degree to which the findings can be applied to other contexts and settings; consistency is concerned with identifying and tracking variability; and neutrality refers to the idea that the findings are solely attributed to the experience of the informants and not to other causes or influences. Emphasis will depend on the type of qualitative design, and the researcher will use a range of different techniques to demonstrate the criteria. For example, in demonstrating the credibility of a study, the researcher may use a combination of techniques such as prolonged engagement in the field; reflexivity through a field journal; triangulation of material; and particular interview styles. The concept of trustworthiness is important in assessing qualitative research processes and in the ethical positioning of the inquiry. However, it can clearly be understood in a number of ways, and some researchers, as we have seen in Chapter 4, prefer to use the term 'rigour'. Nonetheless, the establishment of parameters which are adhered to remains a crucial part of qualitative researching and of constructive and critical appraisals.

Clearly, the understanding and agreement about research methods and approaches enable a process of trust in the research claims and findings, but any research only tells part of the story. The application and implementation of research findings are usually qualified with statements about the 'best available evidence' or current knowledge at the time of implementation. Positivist, scientific empirical research in the postmodern era does not present findings as being conclusive, exclusive and indicative of a singular reality, although arguments regarding the levels of evidence still bestow research privilege.

In considering what counts as evidence for the existence of a particular phenomenon, Denscombe (2002) and White (2009) suggest that this is a fundamental consideration for all researchers, irrespective of the type of research they are undertaking. Clear concept definition and development in qualitative studies have equal status to indicators and variables that are measured or counted in quantitative studies. 'The key consideration is what counts as evidence for the existence of a particular phenomenon, not whether numeric values are to be assigned to cases for the purpose of analysis' (White, 2009: 101).

Finally, and perhaps most importantly, in considering the trustworthiness of research, the integrity of research studies must be assessable not only by the research community but also by potential consumers of the research.

CRITICAL THINKING AND THE RESEARCH PROCESS

When appraising research reporting it is important to bring critical thinking to the task. Descriptive clarity needs to be complemented by a coherent argument that is described by White (2009: 112) as 'a transparent and valid chain of reasoning between the available evidence and the conclusions drawn'. Such an argument leads the reader to a judgement that the claims made by the researcher (that is, the answers to the research question/s) are adequately supported by the evidence presented. This is referred to as the 'warrant' of the study that must be evident in all research, irrespective of the paradigm or method. Warrant is not evidence or the stated research claims, but the argument that links them coherently and persuasively together (Gorard, 2002: 136). They are principles of reasoning that may be evident in different forms depending on the type of research. Some researchers call this 'joining the dots' to form a picture which is not evident in the individual examination of the elements. In social science research, arguments are likely to be explanatory, draw on more than one source of evidence and often acknowledge other plausible interpretations. As discussed in Chapter 7, in empirical, experimental studies the warrant is more explicit, that is, x will lead to result y for these reasons.

The critical appraisal of research may also draw on theorized approaches to critiquing research studies and their findings. Language and discourse are fundamental in appraising research. Drawing on theories such as post-structuralism, feminist perspectives and interpretivist approaches may lead the critical reader to interrogate the use of language in the expression of the research question, concepts, variables and indicators developed for the study. Where research is being undertaken as a problem-solving activity, the way in which the phenomenon being investigated has been 'problematized' to support a particular type of methodological approach is an important element in this review.

Writers such as Gardner (2006) and Bacchi (2009) have developed a series of questions to be considered when taking a critical, discursive approach to the way in which phenomena have been constructed or understood for the purposes of the research exercise. These are similar to the exploration questions suggested by Alston and Bowles (2012) and D'Cruz and Jones (2014), discussed in Chapter 2, that are part of the initial engagement with any research activity. They are the 'who, what, why and how' questions.

In considering the construction of a problem, for example, Gardner (2006: 149) suggests the following questions:

Who sees it as a problem?

What variety of views are there?

What specifically do people want to consider?

What are the underlying assumptions and values?

Why has it come up as an issue now?

What is the history of this issue?

Is there a range of views about the background? What impact does that have on how the issue is now being seen?

In linking these questions to Chapter 4 and the ontological positioning of studies, we would suggest that a further question needs to be considered here that relates to the positioning of the researcher themselves. Critical reflection concerning their own 'world-view' about the phenomenon being considered is also a crucial part in appraising the research.

In an approach used to analyse the 'problematization' process used in policy development, Bacchi (2009) has developed six questions known as the 'What's the problem represented to be?' framework. This framework can be adapted for wider use in the critical appraisal of research by replacing the word 'policy' with the word 'study'. The framework questions would then be:

What is the problem represented to be in a specific study?

What presuppositions or assumptions underlie this representation of the problem?

How has this representation of the problem come about?

What is left unproblematic in this problem representation? Can the problem be thought about differently?

What effects are produced by this representation of the problem?

How/where has this representation of the problem been produced, disseminated and defended? How could it be questioned, disrupted and replaced?

In a similar way to the questions posed by Gardner, the researcher's world-view, values and perspectives will also be brought to bear in the construction of concepts and research design, and these in turn have a direct bearing on the critical appraisal of the research.

Policy and research findings are routinely used to justify actions and interventions that have been legitimized by the use of a 'scientific' approach. Adapting and using the examples of frameworks suggested by Gardner and Bacchi can assist in the critical appraisal and interrogation of research claims in the wider context of nuanced social experience and meaning-making.

Other aspects of research reporting that require critical appraisal include statements about the limitations of the study and the significance of the study.

Turning first to limitations, all research, irrespective of its type and purpose, has limitations that must be clearly articulated as part of research reporting. The ethical approval of research proposals usually requires researchers to explicitly identify the limitations of the proposed study. Once the study has been completed, the presentation of research findings must address both the anticipated and actual limitations. Limitations usually fall into the areas associated with the study design, the study process and the stated claims of the findings. Perceived or real conflicts of interest of those associated with the research and the research outcomes may also be a limitation. Large randomized controlled drug trials funded by pharmaceutical companies and the patents of scientific discoveries are good examples of this, and these relationships must be explicit and accurately documented in research reports and publications to indicate any potential bias or influence in the study findings. While these examples tend to be obvious limitations, other limitations may be more subtle; for example, the relationships of power between the researchers and those being researched may also be a perceived or real limitation of a study. This does not mean, however, that studies are discounted, rather that their integrity is weighed up against the identified limitations and the way in which these limitations were managed, minimized or overcome in the conduct of the research.

Turning now to the significance of the study, it is important when appraising research reporting that the claims regarding the findings or results are realistically stated consistent with the aims and scope of the study and the methodology and research design. One pitfall in research is making claims about the generalizability of the study results more widely than the study warrants. In some research endeavours the results are not what was expected. The results may not support the hypothesis or the findings might require a reinterpretation of the research question. Was it the wrong question? What does a disproved hypothesis actually mean? Dodd and Epstein (2012) suggest that, as part of the task of data interpretation, other possible explanations and understandings of results in comparison to the findings of other studies in a similar field become significant, as does a return to the literature review and the context of the study. 'More generally, it is important to think about possible explanations when the results were not as you would have predicted, and/ or when the results are "not significant" statistically speaking' (p. 186). Supporting this point further, they refer to the work of Yegidis and Weinbach who suggest that both significant and not significant findings 'can be equally valuable' (Yegidis and Weinbach, 2008: 270).

In basic research as well as in applied research, a finding that is not statistically significant is still a finding, though in the former it tends to receive less attention than in the latter. They go on to suggest that in practice-based research studies it is particularly important to differentiate statistical significance and 'social significance' where a statistically insignificant finding may be very significant for practice. Following on from this, an inconclusive study may not be included in a systematic review of the literature, but its significance may be in the articulation of new areas of research including new concepts for further investigation.

CONSIDERING RESEARCH REPORTS – STYLES AND IMPACT

In appraising research it is important to differentiate between the process of appraisal as a systematic activity to test its trustworthiness and the critical appraisal of the research claims drawing from a critique of the values, construction and interpretation of the phenomenon, problem or situation being studied.

The academic tradition of appraising research theses provides one approach to reviewing research and the intellectual scholarship that has been undertaken. Several broad criteria are routinely used that collectively support the overarching theme of the contribution of the research to knowledge building and knowledge creation. These criteria include the adequacy of the literature review as a critical examination of available literature in the field of inquiry; the suitability of the methodology and research design to address the research questions; the clear presentation of evidence to support the stated claims of the findings; the internal coherence of the arguments that lead to statements about the findings; and the potential for publication in peer-reviewed journals and books. However, although these are specifically articulated criteria, they contain implicit subjectivities that are brought to the review and examination task (Denicolo, 2003).

A similar approach is used by technical, scientific and professional journals to assess manuscripts for publication. This is done through a blinded, peer-review process that draws upon these criteria being applied by experts in the field. Whilst objectivity and independence are highly valued, the appraisal of knowledge building and the research process in recent decades has occurred within the wider neoliberal context of the marketization of teaching and learning and the economic influences on research priorities and expectations (Olssen and Peters, 2005). Writers such as Barnacle (2005) refer to the growth and influence of the 'knowledge economy', where knowledge is objectified as a product or commodity in direct contrast to philosophical approaches to knowledge where knowledge is transformational and where there are elusive relationships between the known, the knowing and the knower (Kierkegaard, 1985; Lyotard, 1992; Heidegger, 1993, as cited in Barnacle, 2005).

Another criterion for appraisal is the literature review. Once again the appraisal of the review can be undertaken using a range of different tools, each of which aims to systematically appraise the literature; to identify what is currently known about the topic; the gaps in the existing literature; and the way in which the current study will contribute to the development of new understandings and knowledge. Boote and Beile (2005) have adapted earlier work by Hart (1999) to develop a helpful scoring rubric for this task that contains five key features:

- Coverage, where justified criteria for inclusion and exclusion are clearly presented;
- Synthesis, which includes interrogation and integration of literature;
- Methodology, where research methods have been reviewed and the appropriateness of the selection is clearly evident;
- Significance, where the practical and scholarly significance of the work is clear;
- Rhetoric, where the review has been coherently argued and clearly developed (Boote and Beile, 2005: 8).

As highlighted in Chapter 4, literature reviews can be part of a wider research inquiry or can be undertaken as stand-alone activities. Most peer-reviewed technical, scientific and professional journals will publish literature reviews if they meet specific criteria in terms of content and presentation. Literature reviews that are evidence-based and have a meta-analysis component are referred to as systematic reviews. Systematic reviews are a summary of the best available evidence on a specific topic. Studies included in a systematic review must have specific inclusion and exclusion criteria and an explicit research strategy with findings related to the research question. Studies reviewed include published and unpublished reports and are subject to systematic coding and analysis, with a meta-analysis being undertaken where possible to draw specific conclusions about the results as usable evidence.

Some examples of reporting approaches for systematic reviews are 'Preferred Reporting Items for Systematic Reviews and Meta-Analyses' (PRISMA: Moher et al., 2009) and the *Handbook for Systematic Reviews of Interventions* published by the Cochrane Collaboration (Higgins and Green, 2011). These approaches are often used by professional journals in peer-reviewing literature reviews submitted for publication.

In the field of social care knowledge specifically, the Social Care Institute for Excellence (SCIE) has developed guidelines for systematic reviews (Rutter et al., 2013). A full account of the developmental work underpinning these guidelines can be found in the work of Pawson, Boaz and others with particular reference to the five types of knowledge sources – organizational knowledge, practitioner knowledge, policy community knowledge, research knowledge and user and carer knowledge – and their systematic appraisal using the TAPUPAS framework – transparency, accuracy, purposivity, utility, propriety, accessibility and specificity (Pawson et al., 2003, 2005; Boaz and Pawson, 2005; Sharland and Taylor, 2006).

In the appraisal of all research reporting, whether it be a publication, a report, a policy document or more informal communication, the way in which the research is reported on is crucial when considering its usefulness and application. This is true irrespective of whether it is the latest scientific discovery, a narrative inquiry into a social phenomenon, a case study or an evaluation report. If the research is not written up in a way that enables the reader, consumer or reviewer to appraise its trustworthiness as a study, then the findings lose veracity and may be discounted or set aside. In literature reviews and systematic reviews the findings can be challenged if the research reporting omits information, is unclear about methodology, or the overall rigour of the study is not evident. The presentation of the literature must be consistent with the research orientation, the research design and the methodology. In the social sciences, which draw less on randomized controlled trials but still require systematic appraisal and use of the literature to inform the study, the literature review must reflect the theoretical lens through which the research is being undertaken, including the research design, the formulation of the research questions and the interpretation and analysis of the data. In research reporting the literature review also becomes part of the context of the findings and needs to be revisited by the researcher as part of the interpretation of the findings and statements about significance.

EVIDENCE-BASED PRACTICE – OPPORTUNITIES AND CONSTRAINTS

Evidence-based practice can be traced back to the evidence-based medicine (EBM) movement that emerged after the Second World War in Britain. The aim of EBM was to ensure that all medical practice was based on the 'best available evidence' obtained from the systematic review of research. The Cochrane Collaboration[1] remains the leading group of the EBM movement and was named after British epidemiologist Archie Cochrane (1909–1988), who advocated the use of randomized controlled trials as a means of reliably informing medical practice. Cochrane and his supporters were particularly interested in the reasons why clinicians practised the way they did. Anecdotally, it seemed to Cochrane and others that when doctors were asked why they practised in a particular way the most common response was 'that is the way I was taught to do it'. Cochrane and others realized that there

---

[1]http://www.cochrane.org/

may be differences between university approaches and ways of training and there was no methodical process of integrating new knowledge into medical practice.

In contrast, contemporary clinicians may reply to the same question slightly differently. Anecdotally again, the reply would still be 'that is the way I was taught to do it', but with the additional comment 'that is what the research or evidence tells me'. In clinical practice, where presenting symptoms can be diagnosed and treatment given, EBM has been embraced as a means of improving the standards and quality of clinical intervention.

In EBM, levels of evidence provide a scale of empirical reliability, with randomized controlled trials being classified as the gold standard. In the last three decades, as other health professions have embraced EBM, the term has been widened to evidence-based health care or evidence-based practice (EBP). In keeping with the original approach, levels of evidence for interventions in EBP are still presented as a hierarchy, with randomized controlled trials at the top, followed by quasi-experimental studies, correlational studies, qualitative studies and case studies.

Although there were clear benefits in this approach for science-based professions which undertook clinical interventions, it was problematic for professions where intervention and action were based on 'reflective, interpretive and humanist responses to the personal and social conditions encountered in practice' (Plath, 2006: 57). Increasingly pressures were brought to bear on these professions to demonstrate the effectiveness of practice interventions drawing on the hierarchy of evidence. Unlike clinical interventions that were in response to a diagnosed condition, practice in these sectors was not context- or value-free and actions were based on a range of information, interpretations and understandings. Notwithstanding the arguments about levels of evidence, these approaches could, however, be interrogated and critically appraised. In response to the EBP movement, mixed method approaches, systematic reviews and literature reviews have been used to develop and test theories for practice and for understanding social phenomena. These approaches have resulted in a middle-ground position of research-informed practice that Plath suggests is the way forward to ensure the incorporation of research into practice and about practice.

The recognition of the importance of mixed methods to aid understanding and improve the relevance of research has resulted in the expansion of the role of groups such as the Cochrane Collaboration to include qualitative and mixed method studies applying systematic appraisal of the research findings. The evidence-informed approach has widened to other fields with other groups being established, based on the Cochrane model, for example the Campbell Collaboration[2] that undertakes systematic reviews on the effects of interventions within the areas of education, crime and justice, social welfare and international development.

---

[2]http://www.campbellcollaboration.org/

Adopting a similar approach, some centres have been established for specific professional groups; for example, the Joanna Briggs Institute[3] (University of Adelaide) is a research repository for practice guidelines with a focus on clinical interventions, particularly for nursing and the allied health professions. In the UK, the SCIE[4] systematically reviews and publishes the available evidence in research and policy areas in social care fields and produces guidelines for practice for practitioners in those fields.

Many of the review groups that now work globally as part of these collaborations have interdisciplinary membership including professionals from health, social care and education fields, for example. This interdisciplinarity has widened the scope of systematic reviews, enabling the process to be applied to differently formulated topics and fields including issues of concern, services, policies and practice.

To illustrate the usefulness and limitations of evidence-based approaches and systematic reviews, an example of an area of practice – home visiting of women, babies and pre-school children – will be considered, drawing on Cochrane Collaboration, Campbell Collaboration and SCIE reviews.

―――――――――――― **Researcher Reflection 8.1** ――――――――――――

Systematic reviews and meta-analyses: Cochrane Collaboration and Campbell Collaboration

Home visits during pregnancy and after birth for women with an alcohol or drug problem

Members of an interdisciplinary team comprising a neonatologist, social workers and psychologists working in neonatology were interested in reviewing research that had been undertaken investigating the effectiveness of home visiting for women with a history of substance misuse during pregnancy and after birth. This interest had emerged from their practice. Following the protocol for completing such a review, 150 studies were identified, but only three met the inclusion criteria for review. The review did not prove one way or another that a home visiting programme improved the health outcomes for women in this situation. The systematic review concluded: 'There is insufficient evidence to recommend the routine use of home visits for pregnant or postpartum women with a drug or alcohol problem. Further large, high-quality trials are needed' (Turnbull and Osborn, 2012: 1).

However those studies reviewed did show a reduction in the use of child protection services and the levels of parental stress in those women receiving home visiting. New research in this area will continue to be reviewed by this team and become part of the

(Continued)

―――――――――

[3]http://joannabriggs.org/

[4]http://www.scie.org.uk

(Continued)

Cochrane database. Further research has been suggested which aims to prove the merits or otherwise of a home visiting programme.

The Cochrane Review can be found at:

http://onlinelibrary.wiley.com/doi/10.1002/14651858.CD004456.pub3/abstract;jsessio nid=E96ABAC13352764C65138AAFC62441B0.f03t01

Illustrating the importance of keyword and field searching in these databases, a search of the Campbell Collaboration found a systematic review on 'Home Based Child Development Interventions for Pre-School Children from Socially Disadvantaged Families'. A systematic review and meta-analysis of studies was undertaken and summarized in the review abstract:

> The early years of a child's life are extremely important in terms of development and growth. Children from a deprived family background are at greater risk of developmental problems and poor health. Parenting and the quality of the home environment can help boost young children's development and reduce the negative consequences of deprivation. The purpose of this review was to look at whether home-based parenting programmes, which aim to improve child development by showing parents how to provide a better quality home environment for their child, are effective in doing so. Seven randomised controlled trials ... met the inclusion criteria for this review. It was possible to combine the results from four of the seven studies, which showed that children who received the programme did not have better cognitive development than a control group. Socioemotional development was measured in three studies but we could not combine this data to help reach a conclusion about effectiveness. None of the studies measured adverse effects. The quality of the evidence in the studies was difficult to assess due to poor reporting. More high quality research is needed. (Miller et al., 2012: 5)

In an analysis of the agreement or disagreement of their review with other reviews they noted the following:

> The common view is that home visiting is an important tool in providing support, education and guidance to parents of young children. Home visiting has been shown to improve the quality of the home environment ... and there is some evidence to sup-port the effectiveness of one-to-one and group parent training (for teenage mothers) in improving parent–child interaction ... and emotional and behavioural outcomes for the children ... . This review had a very specific focus on programmes that were child development oriented, however it was unable to support or go beyond the evidence provided by other studies and reviews to provide reliable evidence of their effective-ness in improving developmental outcomes. (Miller et al., 2012: 29)

The study referred to another systematic review completed by Kendrick et al. (2000) that cautiously concluded that home visiting programmes were associated with an improve-ment in the quality of the home environment.

The Campbell Review is co-listed with the Cochrane Collaboration and can be found at http://campbellcollaboration.org/lib/project/190/

In these two reviews a number of points need to be considered. They have reviewed different types of home visiting intervention, resulting in two different domains. Similarities can be found in the technical approaches to the reviews. Both reviews indicated that there were few studies that met the inclusion criteria for meta-analysis, and conclusions were cautious and tentative. Both studies also conclude that more research was needed.

Researcher Reflection 8.2

Evidence-informed practice: SCIE

In looking for further evidence on this topic, a search of the SCIE database located an SCIE research briefing on 'Parenting capacity and substance misuse' (published in 2004 and updated in 2005). The paper is presented with some key messages for practice that have been informed by the available evidence. These key messages are:

The misuse of drugs and/or alcohol may adversely affect the ability of parents to attend to the emotional, physical and developmental needs of their children in both the short and long term

A number of policy and practice documents are available governing the provision of services to support parents who misuse substances

Research has tended to focus principally on substance misusing mothers rather than fathers, and drugs rather than alcohol. Residential programmes which include the children have been demonstrated to be effective

Studies often fail to evaluate the impact of substance misuse on parenting capacity relative to other aspects of disadvantage, such as poverty, unemployment or depression

Parents are worried about losing their children, so confidentiality is considered to be a requirement for support services

Children often know more about their parents' misuse than parents realise, and feel the stigma and shame of this misuse, but also fear the possibility of being separated from their parents and taken into care

SCIE Research Briefing 6: Parenting capacity and substance misuse can be found at:

http://www.scie.org.uk/publications/briefings/briefing06/index.asp

In considering the systematic reviews undertaken on home visiting as part of practice, the evidence for practitioners is clearly not 'gold standard'; however, there is sufficient information provided to draw the conclusion that home visiting should be continued and that there are likely to be some positive outcomes. In a further appraisal of the use of evidence to inform social understandings and also practice, there are other considerations that need to be taken into account. If we return to the ontological positioning of this phenomenon that has led to the development of a 'social issue', we need to ask further questions that go to the values and context that underpin the studies.

These studies review the relationships between mothers and children, particularly newborn children. Social values are both explicit and implicit in the ways in which motherhood, parenting expectations and so on have been developed in the study design. If researchers were drawing from world-views that were underpinned by feminist perspectives discussed in Chapter 4 then the investigation of these relationships between mother and child might be investigated differently. Theoretical perspectives on the ethics of care, the role of parents and the social values and contexts of family life might also influence the research design. In the Campbell Collaboration example, a degree of recognition was given to the limitations of linking evidence-based interventions with problem-solving when discussing the implications for practice: 'It is recognised, however, that such interventions, even when effective, are not a panacea and are insufficient in and of themselves to eradicate inequalities in early development (Burger, 2010). Any contribution of such interventions should be considered within the wider political and economic context' (p. 30).

In recent years there have been calls for social work and other professions in the health and social care sector to adopt EBP to demonstrate the scientific basis of the interventions and practice. However, this is problematic for professions where practice is always contextual and based on many factors that include theoretical perspectives but also other elements such as the values that underpin a situation and those people in it. Ultimately these professions cannot state that a presenting problem or issue should be dealt with in the same way on every occasion.

However, EBP has features that are required and expected of all contemporary professional practice: 'Evidence-based practice indicates an approach to decision making which is transparent, accountable and based on a careful consideration of the most compelling evidence we have about the effects of particular interventions on the welfare of individuals, groups and communities' (Macdonald, 2001: xviii).

The responsibility for all practitioners, researchers and educators is to maintain currency in the most up-to-date information in their field of practice. However, even with the availability of such a wide range of information for practice, professional practitioners must still approach the complexities of their work drawing on a range of knowledge for practice that goes beyond available information. Knowledge for practice encompasses theoretical, empirical, procedural, personal and practice wisdom knowledge (Drury Hudson, 1997) and is the synthesis of all knowledge forms in relationship with judgement, reflexivity, critical reflection and creativity (Taylor and White, 2000, 2006; Fook and Gardner, 2007). In considering social work in particular, Plath (2006: 66) states:

Regardless of how strong the evidence for a particular intervention may be, social workers are in a position where they need to critically reflect on their work in the political, social, organizational and interpersonal contexts, engage in debates, negotiate appropriate practices and when necessary, argue convincingly for the effectiveness of the work being done.

In drawing this section to a close, we will revisit the emergence of practice-based research, discussed in Chapter 2, and its relationship with evidence. Earlier in this chapter, we identified the search for relevance in research as being one of the key drivers of the PBR movement. Issues of relevance are still apparent in a perceived gap between 'top-down' approaches that integrate research knowledge. These perceived gaps have spearheaded the emergence of a PBR movement where a 'bottom-up' approach is privileged and where knowledge is generated from researching practice.

Drawing on the work of Epstein and Blumenfield (2001) and Dodd and Epstein (2012), the differences in approach between evidence- or research-based practice (EBP/RBP) and practice-based research, with particular emphasis on knowledge integration and the role of the practitioner, can be understood. In particular, PBR is viewed as participatory and empowering for the researcher. The differences are summarized in Table 8.1, which identifies the features of each approach and the different ways that knowledge is integrated with practice. EBP/RBP have a more linear relationship where research is integrated *to* practice, whereas PBR approaches have a more immersed relationship where research is integrated *in* practice.

Table 8.1. The differences in approach between evidence- or research-based practice (EBP/RBP) and practice-based research (PBR) and the integration of research knowledge. (Based on the work of Epstein and Blumenfield (2001) and Dodd and Epstein (2012))

Evidence/ Research-Based Practice	Integration of Knowledge Research-to-Practice	Practice-Based Research	Integration of Knowledge Research-in-Practice
A 'top-down' model	Randomized controlled trials and meta-analyses	A 'bottom-up' model	Single case studies
Often external to practice	Standardized quantitative measures	Derivative – from practice	Direct qualitative observation
Research becomes a tool of practice	Researcher-driven	Practice is the object of research	Practitioner-driven
Theories are applied to practice	Practitioner is a research consumer	Theories and concepts emanate from practice	Practitioner is a practice knowledge producer

In presenting the approaches in this way, care needs to be taken not to repeat the errors of past dualisms and dichotomies. Mixed methods can be used successfully in PBR, drawing on the strengths and appropriateness of the range of research techniques and design.

CONCLUDING REMARKS

All readers and consumers of research need to approach the task of constructively and critically appraising research with some key elements in mind. The rigour of the research design and method must be clearly evident, but, in addition, research and research outcomes must demonstrate wider features of trustworthiness and relevance for the contemporary situation. For all readers and consumers of research, the relationship between research, practice and evidence underpins all research endeavours. Ideally, this relationship should be one that is inclusive, participatory and negotiated between opportunities, approaches, contexts, values and meaning-making in knowledge development and its purposeful application.

III
The impact of research

NINE

Research dissemination, sustainability, making a difference and writing for publication

Making a difference is the key purpose of research. However, this is an area often paid insufficient attention at the outset. In this chapter ways of making a difference, sustaining a research culture and strategies for the promotion and dissemination of research findings are explored. Writing for publication is also discussed, looking at some practical steps and achievable goals for early-career researchers.

MAKING A DIFFERENCE FROM THE OUTSET

Most researchers are hopeful that their research findings will have significance and will make an impact as a result of their exploration and investigation of a particular problem or issue of concern. However, 'significance' and 'impact' will largely depend on who *knows* about the research. Thus the dissemination of research needs to be a crucial part of the research activity. For the majority of researchers, it is also probably true to say that once the immense and all-consuming tasks of the research project itself are completed, thoughts of disseminating the findings in the public domain are often left until last or not prioritized for completion. For others, the systematic dissemination of research findings may be a requirement by those funding or commissioning the research. Sometimes imperatives to report may also be seen as a 'tick the box' activity rather than an opportunity to contribute to the public discourse in the field. However, if we return for a moment to earlier chapters where we considered the reasons for undertaking research, then clearly the dissemination of research findings is a necessary and vital responsibility of researchers.

If this is the case, we need to consider why many researchers regard the dissemination of research findings as such a challenge. This may be due to a number of reasons, including a lack of confidence in writing about the project, or the ability to 'defend' the research should it come under scrutiny by external parties or those with perceived 'greater' expertise in the field. Researchers may also hold a perception, rightly or wrongly, that others may not be interested in the findings. Another key reason is the failure to develop a publication and dissemination plan at the commencement of the research as an integral part of the research programme.

The importance of research dissemination is twofold. Firstly, the findings of research may lead to significant improvements and changes in practice, and the circumstances and situations in which individuals, groups and communities find themselves. If these changes are to occur in a timely and expeditious way then research findings need to be disseminated widely and with maximum impact. Secondly, an inclusive approach to the dissemination of research findings may provide new and different audiences for the work, further widening these aspects. No longer the exclusive domain of a privileged and objectified discourse, research findings can be creatively disseminated, incorporating participants, communities and individuals as actors in the sustainable implementation of changes and improvements.

The more traditional methods of research dissemination include:

- Research reports (usually required by funding bodies or those commissioning a study)
- Publications in peer-reviewed professional, academic and technical journals
- Books
- Book chapters
- Conference papers and posters
- Newsletters, e-bulletins, 'in-house' research forums

For those undertaking research as part of a university higher research degree, the dissemination of research may include all of these activities in addition to the completion of a dissertation or thesis that is externally examined by experts in the field.

Examples of the style and content of formal research reports are well documented by most research texts (for example, Gabriel, 2010: 449; Alston and Bowles, 2012: 297). A synthesis of this content in relation to reports, issues papers and policy documents is given in Table 9.1.

In Chapter 3 we noted that ethics approval for research usually includes a requirement that researchers provide a summary of the research findings to participants. This can be discretionary and may include a full copy of the report, a copy of the findings or a summary report. Returning to the theme of inclusivity, questions guiding the report writer may include: Is the report accessible in terms of its language and availability? If appropriate, and depending on the research design and methodology, were participants involved in the writing up of the report and the interpretation of the findings? It is more likely that key

Table 9.1 Usual content of formal research reports, issues papers and policy documents

Research Reports	Issues Papers	Policy Documents
Title page/authorship/funding bodies/affiliations	Title page/authorship/funding bodies/affiliations	Title page/authorship/funding bodies/affiliations
Table of contents	Table of contents	Publication details Recommended citation
Abstract	Introduction	Acknowledgements
Acknowledgements	Literature review	Table of contents
Introduction	Summary of research and findings	Executive summary
Literature review	Issues questions for consultation	Recommendations
Methods	Information about how to provide feedback on issues questions	Introduction
Results	Time lines for submission and completion	Literature review
Discussion	References	Summary of research/findings
Conclusion		Process of consultation
Conflicts of interest		Recommendations in detail
Appendices		Conclusion
References		List of submissions received
		References

stakeholders will support future research initiatives if there is active participation in the preparation of the report, with an opportunity to provide feedback about the findings or recommendations.

DEVELOPING AND SUSTAINING A RESEARCH WRITING CULTURE

When most researchers begin to think about writing it is often at the conclusion of a research project. However, opportunities to maximize the dissemination of information about projects really begin in the early stages of project development. Thus when researchers are initially thinking about a research question or project, they should at the same time be considering a writing plan that is of equal importance to other research activities. Ideally, this writing plan should include concurrent writing activities completed in conjunction with other tasks. For example, the early investigation of the literature about an issue of concern, including the analysis of what is already 'known' or understood about a situation or issue, may lead to a discursive article for publication in a formal journal or in a less formal publication such as a newspaper, magazine or online blog.

Writing about research includes much more than simply disseminating the findings of a particular study or project. Other reasons may include to justify further funding; to promote discussion and research inquiry about questions not fully resolved or about new questions that have emerged; to contribute to stages of problem-solving; and to contribute to knowledge building and knowledge creation. Continuous questioning of the ways in which the research endeavour might be improved illustrates the dynamic nature of the research inquiry and supports a research writing culture. Some forms of research have such a continuous process built into the method itself; for example, participatory action research, used extensively in the education field, enables a continuous process of review and integration into classroom practice with ongoing evaluation.

All of these activities are part of what Dodd and Epstein (2012: 186) refer to as 'transformative perspectives' of new knowledge and new understanding. Researchers may believe that their work is not of significance in the wider research domain; however, research findings and writing about research work should be seen as pieces of a jigsaw puzzle that, when combined with the work of others, can lead to iterative shifts and changes in thinking and action. These are further reasons why research findings and writing about research need a wide range of audiences. This is part of having an impact, making a difference and supporting and sustaining change.

Whilst researchers are motivated by scholarly concerns about the integrity and worth of the research, they also need to consider how to disseminate the messages of research more widely to a non-academic audience. The emergence of social media and online reporting has become a contemporary vehicle for researchers and others to disseminate their message far more widely than previously, whether it be the findings of a discrete study; ongoing information about a particular issue of concern; or opportunities to engage in interactive discussions about a variety of topics of interest. In the social media online information can be static, such as accessing and retrieving reports and documents from websites, but can also be interactive in the form of emails, blogs, Twitter feeds, Facebook and so on where like-minded researchers can exchange information and ideas about research topics, issues of concern and so on. Sites of common interest can be either open access or password-protected and can provide a forum for in-depth discussion.

The emergence of social media as a possible vehicle for the dissemination of research findings requires the user to undertake some early assessments of the conversations and narratives of each site and their compatibility and suitability for posting information. Questions involving the scholarly nature of the sites need to be considered, including the standard and quality of the material being posted, whether the sites are moderated and whether experts in the field use them. Following a site for a while may be advisable to establish credibility. Many authors and academics have established Facebook pages that enable online conversations about their work, whilst others have established more sophisticated sites providing information, resources and discussion opportunities about fields of interest with the researcher and others who log in. An example of this is 'This Sociological Life',[1]

---

[1]http://simplysociology.wordpress.com/

an interactive site established by sociologist and author, Deborah Lupton. On this site, health sociology research and discussions can be found with links to other relevant sites. Researchers with similar interests can participate in and contribute to online discussions about issues of concern in the field. Another example is the website known as 'The Conversation'.[2] This site brings together the expertise of high-quality, investigative journalism with academic authors and researchers to critically analyse current issues in such fields as health, science, politics, economics, education and society.

Publishers also have extensive and informative websites with accessible information and resources that, although specifically concerned with their collections, can provide researchers and students with up-to-date information about literature and trends in specific fields. Social media is actively used and online hubs for authors, researchers and readers are available to join; for example, SAGE Connection[3] is an interactive online site set up by SAGE UK, the publishers of this book. A search of the sites of other publishers would result in similar discoveries.

Social media can play a significant role in sustaining discussions and interest in particular fields of work and can bring together global communities of readers, students and researchers (Poore, 2014). It can be used to supplement more traditional methods of dissemination or it can be used as a complete alternative, in its own right, if more traditional methods have not been successful.

WRITING FOR PUBLICATION

Let us now turn to the process of writing itself. Why do we write? Writing as a researcher carries an imperative to disseminate research findings and new knowledge that ultimately is of benefit to service recipients, service users, colleagues, students, policy-makers and other researchers. If we briefly consider the reasons for writing for publication, we may find some answers to the many questions that arise about how to go about this task.

Perhaps some answers may include the following:

- To persuade the reader to take action
- To persuade the reader to accept a particular view
- To express understanding or support for a cause
- To affirm a continuing position
- To establish the author's reputation in a particular field

The answers we choose will in part determine the way we will go about writing for publication.

---

[2]This can be found at http://theconversation.com/au in Australia, and at http://theconversation.com/uk in the UK.

[3]http://connection.sagepub.com/

Like research itself, there are levels of publication exposure for the writing up of findings. Using a research analogy, if we start with the 'gold standard' of publishing, this would include published books, book chapters and publications in peer-reviewed refereed journals. For the early researcher, breaking into this world is a realistic challenge. Gold-standard journals are those with impact factors measured through processes such as the ISI Web of Knowledge Journal Citations Report that appraises scholarly research and the impact factor of journals as an aid to researchers, students and publishers.[4]

Many peer-reviewed journals also provide opportunities for researchers to contribute short pieces of work that are still in development. These are sometimes called brief reports, clinical correspondence or practice reports. Although still reviewed, they are aimed at supporting researchers and practitioners who are early-career writers and can be a useful way for researchers to disseminate preliminary research findings. Many journals also award prizes and other incentives to first-time published authors, student authors or recent graduates, and these are publicized in the journals and on their websites. In these situations authors are competing with others at the same stage in their careers for both publication and prizes.

Other factors to be considered in choosing an appropriate journal for a manuscript include an assessment of whether:

- The manuscript topic meet the aims of the journal and its readership
- There is a consistent conversation or narrative to which the manuscript makes a contribution
- The journal has local, national or international readership and the manuscript will be of relevant interest
- Authors writing on similar topics publish in the journal
- The manuscript meets a call for papers for special or themed editions

Once the journal has been selected, the guidelines for authors should be followed regarding the style, length and submission of manuscripts. Most journals now have logins on the ScholarOne Manuscripts site (formerly known as Manuscriptscentral) where manuscripts are required to be prepared and uploaded in specific formats once an account has been opened by the intending author.

Some further very important considerations for writers include the manuscript title, the abstract and the keywords. Keywords, in particular, locate the work in the wider literature so it is important to think about your own experiences of searching databases for literature – whether some keywords were more important and easily understood than others, for example. Some journals specify the number of keywords and may also include compulsory keywords in addition to the ones you choose for your manuscript.

The manuscript title also needs careful thought. Is it clear what the article is about? Is it clever but obtuse? Does it contain local information or terminology

---

[4]http://wokinfo.com/

unfamiliar to a wider readership? Does the abstract clearly summarize the issues but still encourage the reader to download the entire article?

Once the manuscript is uploaded to the site it is allocated for blind peer review, usually by two reviewers. Depending on the journal this can be a short or lengthy process. Reviewers' comments are then returned by the editor to the author for consideration and may include recommendations for minor revisions, for major revisions, or the manuscript is rejected as unsuitable. Although disappointing when received, constructive criticism leading to an improved article for publication remains the goal. Peer-review processes vary according to journals; however, editors do have a responsibility to ensure that feedback is constructive and balanced. Occasionally a manuscript may be sent to a third reviewer if the reviews are inconclusive or in substantial disagreement.

Many early-career researchers begin their writing careers as co-authors where they have responsibility for a particular section of a manuscript, such as the literature review. A published literature review by Loupis (2013) is a good example. Working as an early-career researcher in the field of stroke rehabilitation, Loupis completed a literature review on the interdisciplinary use of family conferences in rehabilitation. A systematic review of the available literature was completed using the guidelines provided by the Cochrane Collaboration (Higgins and Green, 2011). A discussion of systematic reviews and their presentation as published literature reviews is given in Chapter 8. Writing with others can also include tasks such as contributing to editing, fact checking and referencing. For practitioners, writing with a colleague, with an academic partner, or as part of a writing group, with each member working to their strengths, can all be useful ways to get started on the proposed publication. Finally, when writing collaboratively it is important to write with someone you trust. It is useful to reach agreement about the division of tasks and shared responsibilities, and the order of authorship (whose name will come first); and to decide how you wish to be known, whether by your initials or your full name, although many journals have protocols and conventions for authorship signatures and affiliations.

When writing up empirical research findings it is important to remember that in the search for available research evidence, data need to be presented in ways that make them accessible for systematic review and inclusion in meta-analyses. The need to improve the standards for reporting research evidence has brought together collaborative agreements in the scientific domain regarding the reporting of randomized clinical trials. International scientific consortia have developed agreed checklists for reporting these to facilitate more accurate appraisal and review as part of this process, for example the CONSORT group (Moher et al., 2010). This group has developed Consolidated Standards of Reporting Trials (CONSORT) with an extension for randomized clinical trials involving social and psychological intervention trials. Guidance and checklists are available for writing up qualitative studies from the Cochrane Collaboration (Higgins and Green, 2011), and peer-reviewed journals provide detailed manuscript guidelines for reporting research studies.

Finally, another way to have work formally recognized is through its classification by the Library of Congress. Many practitioners and researchers complete reports that remain part of agency or government collections that are not published. A suggestion for report authors is to consider applying for a Library of Congress number for a completed report which is at no cost and which provides an official identifier for the report even if it is not catalogued as a published work.[5] This process is another way of establishing the report's credibility in the public domain.

Of course, writing is only one way of letting others know about research. For new researchers another way to get started is in small-group presentations, conference papers and conference posters. In a similar way to some peer-reviewed journals, conferences may award prizes for posters and papers for new researchers that can be an incentive to present new work, thus beginning the establishment of a track record for the researcher and for the research itself. The requirements of these formats enable presenters to develop a clear focus and purpose for the presentation by making decisions about the key points they wish to emphasize. A useful first question is: 'What are the three key points I want the audience to know about this work?'

In *talking* about research to any audience, maximizing the impact of the presentation is not only about content but also about matching the style to the requirements of the audience. Thus presentation formats are largely determined by knowing who your audience is. Is it a group of research sponsors or funders? Is it a group of academic experts in the field? Is it a group of practitioners? Is it a group of student peers? Is it a group of participants who were involved in the study or members of a community in which a research study was conducted? The answers to these questions will determine what is presented, how it is presented, the language that is used, the reliance on technical and/or non-technical data, the use of visual material and so on. Generally, for the majority of presentations, statistical data are best presented in visual form such as coloured bar charts and pie charts, and most word-processing software has these features. Rehearsing conference papers and other presentations with friends and colleagues before the event is also a very useful way to obtain feedback to strengthen the presentation.

So far in this chapter we have been mainly concerned with writing about research from the perspective of the writer/researcher. However, when considering the dissemination of research and its subsequent application or utilization, readers of the research also have a key role in appraising its usefulness. As we discuss in Chapter 8, the criteria for constructively appraising research value and trustworthiness will determine the ways in which research findings are used or applied in practice.

In the dissemination of research and in writing for publication, each research tradition involves levels of complexity and sophistication that must ultimately be mastered in the dissemination process. Whether the researcher has undertaken a

---

[5]More information about this process can be found at http://www.loc.gov/publish/pcn/faqs/

quantitative or qualitative study or is drawing on material to present a critical, dis-cursive account of research, writing about research and utilizing knowledge must complement the process of bringing the story together, meeting the elements of critical appraisal.

While writing up empirical research requires a high level of technical exper-tise in the presentation of statistically significant findings and discussion of their implications in ways that can be understood and interpreted by both peer and lay readerships, a different skill set is required when writing up studies that may have socially significant findings. Qualitative studies must clearly provide the context of the study in terms of the overall conceptualization of the area of study, the 'fit' of theoretical framework and research design, and the interpretative lens through which the findings are understood and implications drawn.

However, irrespective of the research orientation, the presentation of research for dissemination must:

- Be coherent
- Be connected to what is already known or understood about the topic
- Have a strong and logical connection to existing literature
- Have internal coherence where the findings and conclusions can be linked back to the data irre-spective of its form (quantitative or qualitative)

Thus in all scholarly writing, the purpose of the study, the theoretical framework and the research design must be clearly stated and the findings must logically follow from the data collected. All that being said, however, not all research will be accepted and recommendations implemented even if judged as being authen-tic and trustworthy. Issues such as the timing of the study, the implications of the findings, funding pressures, policy constraints, differences in philosophical perspectives, values and political influences can determine whether the research itself needs to be accompanied by other strategies to scaffold advocacy and influ-ence policy and practice. Given this reality, it is important to remember that research findings and data can also be used in secondary studies, with further ethics approval if necessary, and that the dissemination of research and research findings and their interpretation may be revisited and may form the basis of new inquiries and new publications.

CONCLUDING REMARKS

Writing is a skill, and like all skills it improves the more often it is undertaken. It would be true to say that many students, who were excellent writers at the time of their graduation, 'forget' how to write once they leave university. For others, writing abilities may become focused differently according to the context of their practice and the demands of their workplace; for example, their writing abilities may be honed on practice reports, briefing papers and policy documents rather than discursive writing. Writing about research has the added element of exposure to intellectual scrutiny of the work by others. This can be a daunting prospect for new writers. Other factors such as time constraints, competing workplace priorities, immersion in the complex world of practice and the realities of personal and family life all encroach on the mindset necessary for critical analysis, reflection and taking stock.

The writing task itself requires commitment, time and patience. It is a creative pursuit that at the same time requires a routine and systematic approach to the presentation of factual information, abstract ideas, synthesis and interpretation. Most experienced writers have developed approaches to the task that reflect individual preferences and styles for handling and managing a creative yet repetitive activity. Some write continuously, others methodically follow a timetable, others work until dawn, and most have their best ideas when they are not sitting in front of the computer but are peeling vegetables or washing their hair. All writers need to be aware of the 'left brain–right brain' phenomenon concerning the relationship between structured thinking and unstructured (and often unanticipated) bursts of creativity and clarity. Leaving a writing task for a while and then returning at a later date is also a useful strategy when difficulties are experienced. Ultimately each writer needs to spend time working out an approach to writing that is good for them. These approaches are always a 'work in progress', just like the document or manuscript being written, but ultimately there is no greater sense of achievement than to see work published and making an impact in a chosen field.

TEN

Common pitfalls and dilemmas

In this chapter, examples and the experiences of the authors will be used to review theoretical, methodological and common pitfalls. These include the implications of not having a clear research question, carrying out research that is too broad to achieve usable outcomes, the consequences of a lack of planning, collecting large quantities of data without a clear idea of what to do with them, having adequate resources and support in place for the researcher, not spending adequate time on proposal development, jumping into data collection, not using a pilot effectively, and dealing with conflicts and disagreements. The importance of building good supervisory and project infrastructure, such as a steering committee, as well as aspects which include critical review and reflection to sustain the project overall, will be foregrounded.

LOOKING FOR PITFALLS AT ALL STAGES OF THE RESEARCH PROCESS

It is important for all those involved in the research endeavour to keep in mind that there is no such thing as the 'perfect' research study – by its very nature, every piece of research has limitations, even those studies that might be lauded as groundbreaking and of great significance. However, whilst acknowledging this it is also important to recognize some of the more common pitfalls that often beset research activities. In this discussion, pitfalls are those situations that may be experienced by the unprepared, unwary or beginning researcher. Dilemmas, on the other hand, are situations where several courses of action may be identified as being possible, plausible, ethical and appropriate in a research study, while only one course of action can be pursued, requiring a decision that ultimately needs to be justified by the researcher.

We have identified a number of common pitfalls and dilemmas that we will discuss briefly in turn. These include the importance of an achievable research plan; undertaking pilot studies; developing research protocols; dealing with disagreement and conflict; undertaking fieldwork and researcher safety; methodological issues; researching ethically; communicating research findings; articulating theoretical frameworks; and theorizing practice and communities of practice.

The research plan

We look at research mapping in Chapter 4. However, research planning is also of crucial importance, and a common pitfall for those considering undertaking research is the absence of a research plan. Many researchers are eager to begin the tasks and activities involved in the project, without having a clearly outlined direction. This may be because they consider a research plan unnecessary. Others may be under pressure to complete the study in the shortest available time and consider the development of a plan too time-consuming. Without a plan, the effective completion of the study will be in jeopardy, as those working on it will not have considered the study in its entirety. The development of a plan is particularly important for researchers working with others to ensure that there is a commonly understood approach. We discussed the importance of this shared and agreed purpose in the discussion about research partnerships and teams in Chapter 2.

A research plan is necessary to guide the work of the research and must follow the research mapping exercise which focuses on clearly articulating the research aims and objectives; the activities to be completed by whom and by when; the time frames and deliverables; and the availability and allocation of resources (see Chapter 4). The research plan is different from the research protocol as it sets out the blueprint for actually conducting or carrying out the research and as such is concerned with the research process. Research plans may be presented in various styles such as text documents or more visual, interactive styles using graphs and tables.

Research maps and research plans are often combined, and an example of a combined research map and plan presented as a text document is one that is prepared as part of an ethics application. Researchers can use the plan to report on annual research activity. An example of a research plan for an ethics application by a part-time research student completing doctoral studies is presented in Table 10.1.

Research plans may also be presented in a visual style, and of these perhaps the most commonly used are Gantt charts. Traditionally used as a management tool, Gantt charts can be successfully adapted and used in research project management and are an easy-to-read visual presentation of the various elements involved in the progress and management of the research project, including the various

Table 10.1 Research timetable presented as part of an ethics application by a doctoral student

Year	Activities
Year 1	Reading widely and gaining research skills and knowledge Development of research proposal Ethics application and approval
Year 2	Recruitment of participants Data collection/fieldwork and preliminary analysis Commencement of thesis write-up (methodology, literature review)
Year 3*	Additional data collection and analysis Continued thesis writing with draft chapters on methodology and literature review completed
Year 4*	Data analysis continuing Continued thesis writing with early drafts of data analysis and findings chapters
Year 5*	Final analysis Completion of full draft of thesis
Year 6	Final drafting and completion of thesis Submission

Years 3–5* If possible, preliminary findings and/or aspects of the study will be presented at conferences or as articles written for peer-reviewed journals

Table 10.2 A simple Gantt chart illustrating research tasks to be completed within a specific time frame

Tasks	July	August	September	October	November	December
Planning						
Design						
Recruitment						
Fieldwork						
Analysis						
Preparation of final report						
Dissemination and publication						

tasks and activities, and the time frames for completion. From the chart, an overview of a project can be obtained quickly and accurately. An example of a simple Gantt chart is presented in Table 10.2.

Specialized tools for developing more sophisticated Gantt charts are produced by various software manufacturers. These can be interactive in design and enable the illustration of more complex relationships between all the elements of the project plan. Some examples of Gantt chart styles can be found at http://www.gantt.com/index.htm.

The development of a research project is like any other major activity – it involves following processes that are understood and explicit along with some that may be more implicit. Accordingly, the anticipation of unexpected events and associated contingency planning are also important tasks. This is often an overlooked aspect of undertaking research. Another common pitfall is not formulating a research plan that is 'doable' in terms of achieving the research outcomes and the milestones along the way that guide this achievement. Unrealistic time frames and a lack of resources, including suitably trained and available research personnel, can have a negative impact on a project. Time frames need to include realistic allowances for the completion of milestones that are driven by others external to the study – that is, where completion is required, but is undertaken by others. Gaining ethics approval from an institutional ethics committee is one such example, and another is making necessary financial arrangements within an organization to manage research grants or funding. Time commitments by others must be factored in to enable realistic time frames to be set down for the completion of the study.

Pilot studies

Piloting the instruments that have been developed for data collection can avoid any pitfalls with the research tools once the research study has begun. In quantitative studies this may include piloting the survey or questionnaire with a small group that is representative of the sample group. Piloting the research tool and then refining it accordingly will ensure its clarity and reliability as a measure of the variables that have been identified for investigation. In studies where data are being gathered from existing databases, an audit or data retrieval tool can be tested for each element of the data being gathered in a trial run of data retrieval. Similarly, in qualitative studies the interview guide to be used for in-depth interviews may be tested in one or two pilot interviews to ensure that the interview will cover the areas that are the focus of the study.

In a similar way to piloting the research tools, full pilot studies can be a useful way to gather preliminary data about a topic or area. The results can be used to refine larger studies and as forerunners to wider research undertakings. Having results from pilot studies can be a useful strategy in seeking research funding as they demonstrate early results and findings and the ability of the researchers to undertake larger studies.

Research protocols

The size and scope of a research study can present a number of pitfalls for new researchers. Most beginning researchers start off with ideas for research that are too large and complex to be developed into viable research projects. Part of the process of research development is to funnel these ideas into more concise elements that can be systematically studied. Adopting this approach will ultimately lead to a sharper focus on one or two key concepts that, when studied systematically, contribute to the wider body of knowledge in a particular field. Working with a research supervisor or mentor can aid this process.

Examples of pitfalls include developing a research protocol that is beyond the capacities of researchers to manage; for example, a proposed sample size may be too large or research participants may be inaccessible. Researchers may aim to use databases that are large and unwieldy or where there may be differences and inconsistencies in inclusion and exclusion criteria. Dilemmas occur when there are differences in definitions of data elements, time periods and in methods of recording and presenting data. These situations require consideration, management and ultimately decisions about what will be used. Some of these situations can be managed by revisiting the aims and objectives of the study; or they may be identified as limitations of the study that locate the research outcomes within the context of what is practically achievable by the researchers.

Researcher Reflection 10.1

Dilemmas created by differences in definitions of data elements, time periods and in methods of recording and presenting data

In a clinical data-mining study undertaken by one of the authors researching 'victim of crime' presentations at a hospital emergency department, a number of databases were accessed for information. These included:

- Patient hospital records, in which episodes of care were coded using the International Classification of Diseases (ICD-10) (World Health Organization)
- Crime statistics for Australia collected by the Australian Bureau of Statistics
- Statistics collected by the New South Wales (NSW) Bureau of Crime Statistics and Research

The researcher faced the dilemma of how to determine who was a 'victim of crime' for the purposes of the study, as the databases either did not use the term at all or had idiosyncratic terminology. The term was, however, used in various government policies and programmes such as the NSW Victims of Crime Bureau.

The dilemma was resolved after reviewing the aims and scope of the study along with a process of consultation with other experienced researchers. A decision was made to use four assault codes from the ICD-10 manual. Patients who presented to the hospital's emergency department with an episode of care falling under one of these four codes were considered most likely to be potential victims of crime. The hospital records of the sample group were then interrogated further. The data collected included whether or not the patient was identified as a victim of crime and whether this could be determined by reading the notes and entries in the hospital record.

(Continued)

(Continued)

This situation reflects a dilemma often faced by researchers when a concept or phenomenon being studied is unnamed or made up of many elements that the researcher needs to understand and define for the purposes of the study. In publishing the study findings, the limitations of the information systems could also be commented upon with recommendations for further consideration (Pockett, 2009).

Dealing with disagreements and conflict

In Chapter 2 we discussed the types of structures and processes that need to be in place to support research teams working effectively. Before a research project begins, brainstorming all the elements of the project can be an effective strategy to ensure the comprehensiveness of the plan. A commonly used tool in this type of activity is the completion of a SWOT analysis of the project (Humphrey, 2005). This involves the identification of the strengths, weaknesses, opportunities and threats to the project by those associated with it. SWOT analysis has been adapted for use in a range of settings including human resources, community development, and as a leadership and management tool. Within the research environment it may be undertaken at the beginning of a project or at various points during the project, particularly if the project is facing either internal or external situations that are affecting the work of the project in some way. Such an analysis can be a useful review exercise, particularly if there are disagreements or

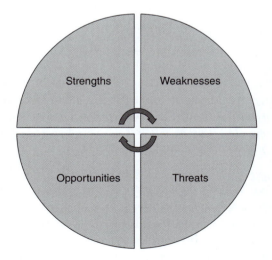

Figure 10.1 Diagrammatic representation of the relationship between elements in a SWOT analysis. Further information on conducting a SWOT analysis can be found at: https://www.tuzzit.com/en/canvas/SWOT_analysis?gclid=CM6H_L2zvr4CFVRwvAod1VkAcQ

differences of opinion about aspects of the project. This type of analysis is also an effective team-building activity for newly formed research teams. The elements of a SWOT analysis are presented in Figure 10.1.

───────────────── **Researcher Reflection 10.2** ─────────────────

Completing a SWOT analysis

Think about a research project you have been associated with and complete a SWOT analysis.

Consider if the elements identified were driven by internal or external factors.

What strategies might be developed to maximize the strengths and opportunities?

What strategies need to be developed to minimize the weaknesses and threats?

In the field and researching safely

A common pitfall for new researchers is either overlooking or not thinking through in detail the logistics and practicalities of conducting fieldwork associated with their research. Fieldwork in ethnographic studies, for example, may involve lengthy observation and immersion in a particular group or community. Exactly how will this be done? What access will the researcher have to the group or community being studied? What resources will be needed to support this engagement? Quantitative studies may require the completion of surveys or questionnaires, and qualitative inquiries may require in-depth interviews with participants – where will interviews be conducted? Are there quiet and private spaces available? How will participants travel to the interview? Will follow-up interviews be possible in the same place? What type of recording will be undertaken? Although these details may seem of lesser importance than some of the more intellectual activities involved in the research task, not giving them the attention they require can lead to difficulties that may threaten the efficacy of the fieldwork and data collection. Thus all those involved in research need to map out these arrangements to support fieldwork activities.

When working in the field, researchers may find themselves in situations that are unfamiliar to them or where they may be at risk of harm. One of the responsibilities of researchers and their supervisors is to ensure that risk assessments are completed and necessary safety protocols and safe behaviours are identified and followed by researchers to avoid any potential harm or distress. Many human research ethics committees require researchers to develop a safety plan or protocol as part of their ethics application if the researchers are considered to be at risk as a result of the nature of the study. Guidelines for the development of such protocols for researchers working away from their usual workplace, in the field or in other countries are usually available with the general information provided to applicants on how to complete their applications. Researcher Reflection 10.3 provides an example of a safety protocol developed by a researcher undertaking in-depth interviews in private homes.

Researcher Reflection 10.3

Safety protocol

The research involves interviews with parents who care for a child or children with high-level care needs and may therefore need to be conducted in private homes. The interviewer will be conducting interviews alone. However, her supervisor considers that the safeguards provided in this safety protocol are sufficient to manage the safety risks.

- Risk-management strategies have been discussed between the interviewer and her supervisor, and both parties are clear as to the procedure. The researcher is experienced in undertaking home visits in a professional (non-research) capacity, including experience in statutory services and as a sole practitioner in non-statutory roles. Her experience includes the assessment of risk and use of protective strategies. The interviewer will discuss interview safety with her supervisor.
- The time and location of the interviews will be communicated to the supervisor. The interviewer will carry a mobile phone and will communicate with the supervisor before commencing an interview and at an agreed time after the interview is completed.
- Where possible, interviews will take place in a public place rather than in a private home. If a home visit is requested by a participant, the interviewer will undertake a telephone assessment to ascertain the safety risk, seeking details such as whether there is street parking at the front of the property, other people expected to be present in the home, presence of animals, etc. All home visits will be subject to the prior approval of the supervisor.
- When an interview takes place in a private home, the interviewer will take steps to ensure that she is able to leave at any time. This includes only entering 'public' areas of the house where possible (such as kitchens and living rooms), ensuring that the exit route is clearly known and clear of obstructions, and watching to ensure that the door is not locked after entering.
- The interviewer will wear clothing that is appropriate to the culture, religion and ethnicity of the participant. Apparel and footwear will allow ease of movement.
- Should anything untoward happen, or if the interviewer becomes uneasy for any reason, the interview will be terminated immediately and the interviewer will leave. The supervisor will be contacted as soon as practically possible.
- Where possible, interviews will be conducted in daylight hours or in the early evening.
- Transport to and from the interview will be by a car that is not the interviewer's own. A pre-booked taxi will be used if a hire car cannot be arranged. On arrival, the car will be parked in the street, facing in the direction of departure.

This safety protocol has been agreed and accepted by the researcher and the supervisor.

Student's signature   Supervisor's signature
Date   Date

(The above safety protocol is reprinted with the permission of Pam Joseph and was developed using the suggested template provided by the University of Sydney Research Office, May 2014.)

Methodological issues

Many of the pitfalls related to methodology have been discussed in previous chapters; however, we will revisit some of the more common ones here.

The research design, theoretical perspectives, context of the study and research questions must 'fit' together. Such 'fit' is often absent when a researcher confuses research orientations to the extent that the research design lacks rigour, leaving it open to scrutiny and questions about its trustworthiness. There are some key intersections in a research project where this may become evident and we will look at four in particular. Probably one of the more common examples is in the sampling process, where quantitative and qualitative sampling methods are inappropriately used. This may occur when quantitative researchers do not achieve the necessary confidence levels in the sample size or qualitative researchers include large samples unnecessarily.

Another key intersection occurs in understandings around objectivity and subjectivity and the role of the researcher; for example, the objectivity required of the researcher in quantitative approaches contrasted with the subjectivities required in qualitative approaches. The last critical intersection is in the development of a research hypothesis or research question that does not reflect the methodological lens of the study. In quantitative research orientations the hypotheses state the variables and their relationship to each other. They set the parameters of the study and the way that data will be analysed. In qualitative research orientations the questions are often developed as a more iterative process that emerges from the field of inquiry or the phenomenon being explored. They also reflect the theoretical framework or lens through which the study will be viewed, the findings interpreted and the positioning of the researchers understood, in relation to what is being studied.

Making claims beyond the scope of the study findings is also a common pitfall, particularly in qualitative studies where generalizability may be misrepresented; for example, a qualitative study exploring six case studies of domestic violence presentations at a community centre may result in an improved understanding of the experiences of those women and their relationship with services at the centre.

Claims that the study has shown that specific services were effective and should be implemented throughout the sector cannot be made. The study findings may, however, have implications for other services and may also warrant further research in some key areas identified in the study.

Researching ethically

While not revisiting the many ethical considerations involved in research discussed in Chapter 3, there are some common pitfalls and dilemmas that need to be identified here. Researchers must continually consider whether their research activities are ethical, and not merely rely on the approval of an institutional ethics committee to make this decision. Once a study has been approved, it must continue to be conducted in an ethical way. Non-coercive practices with participants and all those involved in the research must be followed. Dilemmas may arise around the issue of consent, for example. Is it ongoing or given at a fixed point in time for a particular action? Consent for all aspects of the study may have been obtained at the outset of a study, but there may be circumstances where it needs to be reviewed. In qualitative studies where deductive disclosure is a factor, that is, where the identity of the respondent can be deduced from the qualitative data about their social circumstances, consent may require renegotiation to ensure that confidentiality is not compromised (Tolich, 2004). Ensuring that participants are involved in decision-making about the dissemination of information about them is an imperative of ethical qualitative approaches. Writers such as Kaiser (2009) have suggested some practical ways for the researcher to address these concerns, including the development of a 'post-interview' confidentiality form which 'gives respondents the option to be identified and allows respondents to pinpoint which pieces of data they feel must be handled most carefully' (p. 1638). These approaches are inclusive and participatory and ensure that ethical stances are evident throughout the research process.

Communicating research findings

Completing a piece of research without the final step of publication and dissemination is a common pitfall in research, particularly in the human services sector, and particularly by practitioner researchers, where competing priorities in the workplace often overcome the best intentions for completion. However, with the increasing expectations associated with evidence-based practice and research-informed practice, this must necessarily become part of all research plans. Notwithstanding this imperative, the integration of research into policy and practice has a variable history. Even with publication and active dissemination strategies for research findings, the transfer of research knowledge is slow and in some cases opportunistic. This has led to the emergence of a new 'science', that of knowledge translation (Graham et al. 2006; Barwick et al., 2009). Adopting a similar approach to action research strategies, at the heart of theorizing knowledge transfer, are the circular and interdependent processes of the identification of the problem or issue to be investigated, the inquiry, synthesis, interventions, contexts, barriers and actions. Although circular and interdependent, practitioners may still view this process as one that is externalized from their practice. This brings us to a further dilemma for discussion: can practice be theorized? This is a question that many practitioners and practitioner researchers face when locating their research within the dominant perspectives of what constitutes research knowledge. Along with this question is the further dilemma of articulating the theoretical frameworks that inform the study. We will look at this before turning to a discussion about theorizing practice.

Articulating theoretical frameworks

One of the more challenging aspects of developing a research study is the articulation of the theoretical framework that will inform the study's design and the interpretation of the data. In this book we have reprised three key themes throughout our discussions about research approaches: the importance of world-views or ontological and epistemic frames; inclusivity and participation; and how research can inform policy and practice. These themes are not separate from research orientations but, we argue, should be part of the total fabric of the research endeavour. Beginning researchers often struggle to identify and articulate a theoretical framework for their research, and sometimes this can be perceived as a barrier between academic research and practice research. One way forward is for all researchers to ask themselves some key questions before they start the research:

- What is it that I want to know?
- What is the phenomenon/area or field?
- What do I already know about it?
- How do I feel about it?

An analysis of the answers to these questions usually clarifies how the situation is being understood. This understanding is an implicit mixture of types of knowledge, experience and values of the researcher. Writing and refining the answers can provide a sense of direction in terms of the type of research that the researcher is interested in undertaking. As D'Cruz and Jones (2012: 131) put it, researchers may also reflect on their 'ethical positioning and their socio-political positions'. To illustrate how these views may influence the development of research ideas and the formulation of research questions, they demonstrate the ways in which the explicit or implicit categorization of people can reflect the positioning of researchers and research studies. Some common pitfalls here include categorizing those involved in the research in a negative way, emphasizing their differences or grouping them together as 'a problem' or stereotyped in some other way. Citing an example in Barn (1994), about research concerning black children in foster care in Britain, two examples are given, the first categorizing black children as 'a problem' using the research question 'Why are there so many black children [in Britain] in foster care?' An alternative question in which the category of people is non-discriminatory is suggested: 'What are the processes that involved the entry of black children into care?'

In Chapter 3 we described an example of workplace research at a family support agency illustrating the ways in which world-views underpin research approaches and different orientations. In the following researcher reflection we revisit the workplace to consider the ethical and socio-political positioning of the researchers as suggested by D'Cruz and Jones (2012).

———— Researcher Reflection 10.4 ————

Revisiting the research question

A number of workers in a family support agency continually complain to their supervisors about the lateness of or failure to attend by some clients, blaming this on clients' lack of responsibility; inability to organize themselves; and a lack of respect for the service. The majority of the clients are Indigenous people.

Develop a research question that reflects the categorization of people as 'a problem'.

What ethical and socio-political underpinnings are apparent in posing the research question in this way?

Another group of workers who are experiencing the same problem suggest a review of the engagement of clients with the service by stepping through the experience as a client.

Develop a research question that reflects the category of people in a non-discriminatory and emancipatory way.

What ethical and socio-political underpinnings are apparent in posing the research question in this way?

Theorizing practice

We now turn to the vexed issue facing practitioner researchers and those wishing to research practice: how to theorize their practice in ways that will enable practice-based research to claim its status alongside other more traditional and dominant 'theory/research/practice' relationships. To start we must ask what exactly practice is. It is useful to pause and briefly consider some of the philosophical underpinnings of knowledge and action and the 'practice' that results. Writers such as Dunne (2005), Green (2009) and Kemmis (2005, 2009) have revisited Aristotelian concepts of 'phronesis', 'praxis' and 'aporia' to tease out the nuanced meaning of knowledge for action and the moral dimensions to that action. Paraphrasing the work of these authors, 'phronesis' is a form of action-orientated knowledge that is experiential and understood in wider universal situations and contexts that results in a type of *practical* reasoning rather than the technical reasoning that is based on theories and evidence. 'Praxis' is where thoughts and ideas are used purposefully, with moral intent which may be theoretically informed and drawing on phronesis. Finally, 'aporia' is where situations are complex, unresolvable, paradoxical and ambiguous and require judgement. It is this element of judgement that professional practitioners rely on in their day-to-day practice but which they often cannot articulate or break down into its elements. The work of Michael Polanyi and tacit 'knowing' is also relevant here, where what is known may not be able to be explicated in a technically rational sense (Polanyi, 1967).

The way in which practice evolves is further explored by Kemmis (2005: 392):

> Expert practitioners search not only within their own store of professional practice knowledge for ideas relevant in understanding and acting in particular practice situations, but also within the whole of their own life experience. They search for ways of understanding and acting that will be appropriate in addressing the practical problems they meet at any particular time, drawing on their life-experience not in a static or rationalistic way, but *reflexively*: changing their reading of the situation as it unfolds in and through practice, in the light of changing perceptions, observations and ways of seeing the situation, and in the light of changes brought about by seeing how others see it, and how they are reacting and responding to changes as the situation unfolds.

The use of reflexivity in practice has become the foundation for new approaches that critically analyse the underpinning values, assumptions and world-views that bring about practice actions (Brookfield, 1995; Taylor and White, 2000).

In the literature on critical reflection for practice, key writers such as Jane Fook and Fiona Gardner (2007) have developed these ideas further. Critical reflection draws on four theoretical traditions: reflective practice (see the work of Donald Schön); the concept of reflexivity; postmodernism and deconstruction; and critical social theory (see the work of Michel Foucault and Pierre Bourdieu, for example). Other contemporary social philosophers such as Ted Schatzki have brought many of these strands of thought together in a loose association around practice that involves concepts of 'agency, knowledge, language, ethics, power and science' (Schatzki, 2001: 13–14). The loose connection of these concepts is one way of understanding 'the practice' of professionals.

Critical reflection approaches have been widely adopted by practitioners from many disciplines, particularly in health and social care and education, as a means through which they can better understand troubling issues and seemingly unresolvable practice dilemmas and uncertainties. They involve 'the unsettling and examination of fundamental (socially dominant and often hidden) individually held assumptions about the social world in order to enable a reworking of these and associated action for changed professional practice' (Fook and Gardner, 2007: 20).

The emergent 'changed' professional practice may be viewed as new practice theory to be drawn upon in future practice, thus creating a 'practice/theory/practice' relationship that supports the argument that practice can indeed be theorized for the purpose of research. The challenge for practitioners then is teasing out what they know or experience in practice using the language of research inquiry, turning it into researchable ideas expressed as variables, concepts or phenomena to be studied.

Communities of practice

Turning to some final comments on this process, we need to consider the ways in which forms of knowledge may be further developed by the relationships between those coming together and seeking to explore it. By this we mean interdisciplinary partnerships and communities of practice. In understanding this process, we can refer to the philosophical underpinnings of knowledge creation and the iterative processes of knowledge, action and judgement, and we can also include here the transformative engagement with knowledge from an epistemological stance when those associated with research come together.

Communities of practice are more than professional disciplines working together; they are a means by which knowledge is transformed and re-engaged. Writers such as Couturier et al. (2008) discuss the emergence of communities of practice as a process related to 'interdisciplinarity' where the transformation of disciplines that are 'co-present' and 'co-active' may lead to new knowledge, new disciplines or an internal transformation within each in relation to the other. They suggest two perspectives: one being 'praxeological' and involving a joint effort to manage complexity, drawing on shared disciplinary knowledge and practice; and the other 'epistemological' where the phenomenon under study is reconstructed into a whole entity that is an agreed 'reconceptualization of the whole or a newly formed entity or situation'.

The concrete meeting of disciplines (often through research) fosters the emergence of an 'interdisciplinary discursive space' (Klein, 1996: 220) that allows for the collective formulation of a system of higher-level concepts that are highly prescriptive to the extent that they create and legitimate a way of problematizing that transversely imposes its own necessity of action. This is where practical, academic and scientific interdisciplinarity converge (p. 347).

Some writers refer to this process as one of 'transformation' that involves deep, structural shifts in previous ways of thinking and being (O'Sullivan, 1999; Mezirow, 2000). Other writers such as Kemmis (2005) speak of epistemic, transformative processes that occur in knowledge creation and development through shared experiences. Returning to the work of Dunne (2005), such new and transformative ways of understanding may hold 'epiphanic power', realizing new truths and ways of understanding.

When these transformative processes occur collectively and where those involved may be professionals, clients and others associated with them, communities of practice and new relationships with knowledge are developed.

Thus the practice-based researcher or the researcher struggling to 'theorize practice' is positioned in this process. These approaches are indeed grounded in theoretical knowledge frames about what constitutes practice. Good ideas in practice can become researchable, drawing on a range of research orientations, knowledge frames and world-views in equal partnership.

DEVELOPING EFFECTIVE RESEARCH SUPERVISORY RELATIONSHIPS

Many of the pitfalls and dilemmas that are common in research can be foreshadowed and managed through effective research supervisory relationships. No matter what type of research is being undertaken, it is important to have these relationships established to ensure that the dilemmas that arise in research can be constructively reviewed to facilitate decision-making and provide support and guidance in problem-solving. These relationships can take on various forms such as one-to-one supervision with a research supervisor or mentor, or through involvement in research reference groups.

One of the key elements of research supervisory relationships is that they provide a 'space and place' in which the researcher can engage in reflection about the research project. They can also enable the researcher to critically engage with the topic or issue beyond the practicalities of conducting the research and the epistemological perspectives that underpin it. In the human services sector, research is mainly drawn from the social sciences tradition. Reflexivity or a '360 degree' gaze enables the researcher to question the social and cultural understandings, assumptions and values that may explicitly and implicitly underpin their engagement with the topic or issue and the ways in which they research it. In the context of epistemic and ontological perspectives that shape world-views, an effective supervisory relationship is an essential element at all stages of the research process. In Chapter 2 we discussed the practice supervision relationship as providing fertile ground for the development of research ideas that emerge from the critical engagement with practice. Taylor (2006) believes that practitioners and researchers in health and social care (and, we would argue, in other fields such as education and social policy) share a similar relationship with knowledge and social inquiry, arguing that

> practitioners, just like researchers are implicated in the work in which they are engaged. They do not simply observe in a neutral fashion and gather objective facts about people and their 'problems', they construct versions of cases, and in this sense, make knowledge about patients and service users. (p. 75)

These approaches are important in quantitative approaches too, as they enable the researcher to understand the epistemic construction of the topics and problems they are investigating. This can make a significant contribution to the richness of the discussion by the researcher of the findings, their wider significance and the implications for further research.

Research reference groups or committees are often established to fulfil a similar role. They are usually made up of members who have particular knowledge and expertise in the field of inquiry or who may be members of the community or group where the research is being undertaken. Consumers and service users may also be participants in these groups or committees. In some research fields, reference groups and their membership are specifically mandated, for example research projects involving Indigenous peoples and communities. In these situations, researchers are required to establish and maintain reference groups with community representatives to ensure that the research, at all stages, is conducted in a non-discriminatory and culturally sensitive way. We would argue that their establishment should go beyond an external requirement, however, and be part of the essence of the research itself, as an inclusive and participatory activity. Increasingly, evidence of the existence of well-functioning reference groups is a requirement for the publication of research studies in peer-reviewed journals.

In Chapter 2 we described academic and practitioner collaborations in which practitioners played an important role as members of research reference groups. In these studies, practitioner expertise facilitated access to research participants, provided practice insight into the interpretation of findings and gave general guidance to the progress of the research, thus ensuring the ongoing relevance of the study beyond the more technical considerations. The different perspectives and experiences that members of research reference committees bring to a study can also help to counter any tendencies towards 'group thinking' that may be a danger in projects that run for long periods of time with the same team members. They can also play an important role in ensuring research accountability through challenging and monitoring any perceived conflicts of interest or epistemic bias that may arise or be associated with a study.

BUILDING RESEARCH INFRASTRUCTURE

When we use the term 'infrastructure' we immediately think of the bricks and mortar or physical requirements needed to enable research to be conducted. In the science domain, it is not uncommon for research centres to be located in buildings specially designed for this purpose. In fact the existence of well-resourced laboratories and research centres reinforces the dominant, empirical frame when thinking about research. On the other hand, research in the social sciences, in the wider health field and in education tends to be located in offices, at the desk, in libraries, on-site in agencies and organizations, online and in community fieldwork.

All researchers require a place to do their research, and ideally this needs to occur within a research space where the research is valued, affirmed and supported and where the researcher has a sense of belonging. This may be a real or a virtual space where researchers can form relationships around common interests.

Developing a research culture within an organization can be just as important as the location of physical space. This can be established and supported as part of the goals and objectives of the organization and also as a priority activity by those in leadership positions. The relevance of research to the ongoing activities of an organization needs to be clearly articulated to demonstrate that there are advantages for the organization in supporting it. Thus research purposes can be multiple, and they need to be considered strategically. The value-added component of research to an organization is just as worthwhile as other imperatives may be in undertaking it. Feedback about the research and the dissemination of findings are also an important but sometimes forgotten step in maintaining the communication processes that are necessary within organizations to provide ongoing research support. Finding like-minded colleagues can be an important precursor in building research networks of members with common research interests.

Those in leadership and management positions can also play an important role in establishing a research culture that prioritizes research activities. Organizational and professional leaders need to be receptive to the research needs of the organization at particular times. Sometimes these are opportunities in disguise as they may be vehicles to demonstrate the research abilities and capacities of practitioners in the organization that may then lead on to other research possibilities.

Practitioners who are undertaking research need time and space within the workplace to do this; however, most practitioners are 'time poor'. Strategies that support research cultures include such things as identifying issues of concern through practice supervision that can be shared with others who may be experiencing the same situation; negotiating a roster with colleagues for time away from the workplace 'frontline' to enable practitioners to pursue research activities; building in journal clubs and reading circles as part of ongoing professional development activities; adopting a research-informed practice approach; supporting staff to take students; negotiating research partnerships within the organization and with academics in the field; and encouraging staff to undertake postgraduate and higher research degrees, the progress of which becomes part of the ongoing professional research engagement by all the staff.

Ideally, research groups need a mixture of research expertise and know-how. In this way new members can identify their strengths and feel that they are making a contribution whilst learning other research skills. Two of the more specialized research skills are writing research grant applications and capabilities in statistical methods. Belonging to research networks can be an effective way to find others with particular expertise and skills in the various research tasks and activities. If researchers are working in organizations, it is beneficial to look around as there is bound to be someone who has the expertise that is required. Engaging the skills and expertise of others can foster research networks and collegial approaches to common issues of inquiry where individual researchers work to their strengths, with each making a valuable contribution to the collective, critical mass of research being undertaken. In a more straightforward way, in studies where funding has been received, the research expertise that is required can be supported through targeted recruitment of research personnel with the relevant skills.

CONCLUDING REMARKS

In this chapter we have reprised some of the topics covered in earlier chapters with a specific focus on common pitfalls and dilemmas that may be experienced by researchers. Seeking out research support is an important aspect of the research process. In Chapter 2 we discussed research as a partnership between all those associated with the research inquiry, including the knowledge frames that under-pin the conceptualization of the topic or field of inquiry. Inclusive approaches can aid the design of research inquiries to avoid some common pitfalls. Others can be anticipated and acted upon through supervisory and collegial relationships in communities of practice in research where world-views, knowledge and know-how come together in achievable research undertakings that are both significant and trustworthy, reflecting the research orientation being used.

ELEVEN
Concluding remarks

REVISITING KEY THEMES

In this book we have drawn attention to the vision, creativity and enthusiasm that can go into turning good ideas into viable research questions and 'doable' research projects. We have also highlighted the need for rigour, trustworthiness and attention to detail to turn viable research endeavours into purposeful and productive research undertakings that make a difference.

The three key themes from this book, we believe, forge new horizons in research generally and in practice research in particular. Whatever the orientation adopted, whether qualitative, quantitative or mixed method, we emphasize that attention has to be paid to the world-view held or adopted for a particular research project. This necessitates the concomitant knowledge and theoretical frameworks being subject to ongoing critical appraisal and scrutiny. It is no longer good enough, for example, to claim logical rational underpinnings and to see this as being sufficient justification for carrying out a research project in a particular way. What is understood by 'logical' and 'rational' needs to be explored, examined and used to inform not only the formulation of the research question from the good idea, but also the mapping and planning of the research project, with attention being paid to its overall purpose.

With regard to inclusivity and participation, although we have highlighted that what is meant by these terms in the context of a particular research project has to be clearly defined and that the process requires considerable planning, we have also emphasized throughout this book that it is no longer acceptable to carry out research 'on' subjects. Researching 'with' participants does not constitute a 'one size fits all' approach, but draws attention to changing research ethics and research project requirements. What the research project is likely to mean for those who participate and whether the overarching purpose is one which would generate wide-ranging support have become important considerations.

Similarly, it is crucial to maximize the impact of research in policy to practice and of practice to policy domains by paying attention to key elements associated with underpinning world-views, understandings of knowledge, how to develop research questions, how to select an appropriate theoretical framework, how to integrate theoretical perspectives with empirical research, how to gather and interpret data, and how to operate strategically with regard to policy and practice dissemination. Prevailing ideologies, political expediency, context-specific factors and the extent to which a particular area has generated media and public attention all play a part in policy production and practice formulation; nevertheless, the part that can be played by research should not be underestimated. Clearly, specific research findings can be put forward to justify a particular course of action, and headline findings, dissociated from the underpinning research, can be misleading and dangerous. However, research carried out by practitioners, for example, can change what might have become rigid and counterproductive procedures, can shed new light on old problems and can generate new enthusiasm for change. Ideas, research questions and research projects matter, and a primary purpose of this book has been to encourage more practitioners, service users, women and men, whatever hat they may be wearing, to engage in this dynamic and productive arena.

NEW HORIZONS IN PRACTICE RESEARCH

When we first began to think about this book, we wondered what more could be said about doing research. It is indeed a crowded field of publications concerning the ways to conduct research, in-depth books on methodology and research proficiency, and the minutiae of the task from the first step to the last. In stepping back from what was already available we have endeavoured to present to readers and researchers a process of thinking about research *differently*, creating a new lens through which research can be explored and successfully undertaken. This difference is underpinned by a commitment that research must have clarity of purpose with clear and inextricable links to policy and practice, and must also reflect the moral purpose of the endeavour through epistemological positioning and inclusive and participatory approaches that are woven into research design and evaluation.

Throughout the chapters we have used examples of innovative research that illustrate this purpose, drawing from a number of disciplines and fields of inquiry. In developing the 'researcher reflections' we have aimed to support a transformative understanding of the meaning and processes of undertaking research beyond the surface level of engagement with technical research skills and competencies. Drawing some analogies with the concept of transformational learning (Mezirow, 2000), becoming a transformational researcher means that the researcher has examined in a 'deep' way their taken-for-granted assumptions and frames of reference to engage in new ways of understanding the area which is being researched for the purpose of new meaning-making. These relationships with knowledge and ways of knowing, along with the findings and interpretation of the research outcomes, can then be translated into useful and incisive contributions to policy and practice debates. Research must begin with an original idea and can often result in findings and outcomes that are also unique. Research studies need to be seen collectively as part of a developing and nuanced engagement with the concepts and ideas that have been investigated and explored. Not uncommonly, the most original ideas and outcomes often challenge prevailing beliefs, values and norms. This is true for all research, irrespective of the research design and method. In the contemporary research environment and the competing socio-political context in which all work is now undertaken, the value of the transformational researcher becomes ever more important.

References

Allen, T. (2001) Interpretative biography as a method: Researching tenants' experiences of housing renewal. Unpublished paper, University of Bradford.

Alston, M. and Bowles, W. (2003) *Research for Social Workers: An Introduction to Methods*, 2nd edition. Crows Nest, NSW: Allen and Unwin.

Alston, M. and Bowles, W. (2012) *Research for Social Workers*, 3rd edition. Crows Nest, NSW: Allen and Unwin.

Anderson, M. and Freebody, K. (2014) *Partnerships in Education Research: Creating Knowledge that Matters*. London: Bloomsbury Academic.

Attride-Stirling, J. (2001) Thematic networks: an analytical tool for qualitative research. *Qualitative Research*, 1(3): 385–405.

Australian Association of Social Workers (2010) *Code of Ethics*. Canberra: AASW.

Australian Institute of Aboriginal and Torres Strait Islander Studies [AIATSIS] (2012). Guidelines for Ethical Research in Australian Indigenous Studies [GERAIS]. AIATSIS: Canberra. Retrieved from http://www.aiatsis.gov.au/research/ethics/resources (16 February 2015)

Australian Institute of Health and Welfare and Australasian Association of Cancer Registries (2012) *Cancer in Australia: An Overview 2012*. Cancer series no. 74. Cat. no. CAN 70. Canberra: AIHW.

Bacchi, C. (2009) *Analysing Policy: What's the Problem Represented to Be?* Frenchs Forest: Pearson Education.

Bachman, R. and Paternoster, R. (1997) *Statistics for Criminology and Criminal Justice*, 2nd edition. Boston: McGraw-Hill.

Banks, S. (2001) *Ethics and Values in Social Work*, 2nd edition. Basingstoke: Palgrave.

Barn, R. (1994) Race and ethnicity in social work: some issues for anti-discriminatory research. In B. Humphries and C. Truman (eds), *Re-thinking social research* (pp. 37–58). Aldershot: Avebury.

Barnacle, R. (2005) Research education ontologies: exploring doctoral becoming. *Higher Education Research and Development*, 24(2): 179–188.

Barnes, C. (2001) Emancipatory disability research: project or process. Public lecture, 24 October, Glasgow. Retrieved from http://www.leeds.ac.uk/disabilitystudies/archiveuk/Barnes/ (20 October 2012).

Barnett, R. (2007) *A Will to Learn*. Buckingham: Open University Press.

Barwick, M., Peters, J. and Boydell, K. (2009) Getting to uptake: do communities of practice support the implementation of evidence-based practice? *Journal of the Canadian Academy of Child and Adolescent Psychiatry*, 18(1): 16–29.

Beauchamp, T.L. and Childress, J.F. (2001) *Principles of Biomedical Ethics*, 5th edition. New York: Oxford University Press.

Benhabib, S. (1995) Feminism and postmodernism. In L. Nicholson (ed.), *Feminist Contentions: A Philosophical Exchange*. London: Routledge.

Beresford, P. (2002) User involvement in research and evaluation: liberation or regulation. *Social Policy and Society*, 1(2): 95–105.

Bessarab, D. (2013) The supervisory yarn: embedding Indigenous epistemology in supervision. In B. Bennett, S. Green, S. Gilbert and D. Bessarab (eds), *Our Voices: Aboriginal and Torres Strait Islander Social Work*. South Yarra, Vic.: Palgrave Macmillan.

Bessarab, D. and Ng'andu, B. (2010) Yarning about yarning as a legitimate method in Indigenous research. *International Journal of Critical Indigenous Studies*, 3(1): 37–50.

Best, S. (2012) *Understanding and Doing Successful Research: Data Collection and Analysis for the Social Sciences*. Harlow: Pearson.

Boaz, A. and Pawson, R. (2005) The perilous road from evidence to policy: five journeys compared. *Journal of Social Policy*, 34(2): 175–194.

Bone, S., Vertigan, A. and Eisenberg, R. (2011) Pre-operative assessment of voice abnormalities in patients with thyroid disease: a clinical data-mining exploration of 'thyroid voice'. In R. Giles, I. Epstein and A. Vertigan (eds), *Clinical Data Mining in an Allied Health Organization: A Real World Experience*. Sydney: Sydney University Press.

Boote, D. and Beile, P. (2005) Scholars before researchers: on the centrality of the dissertation literature review in research preparation. *Educational Researcher*, 34(6): 3–15.

Bradshaw, J. (1977) The concept of social need. In N. Gilbert and G. Specht (eds), *Planning for Social Welfare*. Englewood Cliffs, NJ: Prentice Hall.

Brewer, J. (2000) *Ethnography*. Milton Keynes: Open University Press.

Brookfield, S. (1995) *Becoming a Critically Reflective Teacher*. San Francisco: Jossey-Bass.

Bryman, A. (2008) *Social Research Methods*, 3rd edition. Oxford: Oxford University Press.

Burger K. (2010) How does early childhood care and education affect cognitive development? An international review of the effects of early interventions for children from different social backgrounds. *Early Childhood Research Quarterly*, 25(2): 140–165.

Butler, J. (1993) *Bodies that Matter: On the Discursive Limits of Sex*. London: Routledge.

Butler, J. (1995) Contingent foundations. In L. Nicholson (ed.), *Feminist Contentions: A Philosophical Exchange*. London: Routledge.

Butow, P., Ussher, J., Kirsten, L., Hobbs, K., Smith, K., Wain, G., et al. (2005) Sustaining leaders of cancer support groups: the role, needs and difficulties of leaders. *Social Work in Health Care*, 42(2): 39–55.

Bywaters, P. (2013) Inequalities in child welfare: towards a new policy, research and action agenda. *British Journal of Social Work*. doi:10.1093/bjsw/bct079.

Bywaters, P., Brady, G., Sparks, T. and Bos, E. (2014a) Child welfare inequalities: new evidence, further questions. *Child and Family Social Work*. doi: 10.1111/cfs.12154.

Bywaters, P., Brady, G., Sparks, T. and Bos, E. (2014b) Inequalities in child welfare intervention rates: the intersection of deprivation and identity. *Child and Family Social Work*. doi:10.1111/cfs.12161.

Bywaters, P., McLeod, E. and Napier, L. (2009) *Social Work and Global Health Inequalities: Practice and Policy Developments*. Bristol: Policy Press.

Campbell, D.T., Stanley, J.C. and Gage, N.L. (1963) *Experimental and Quasi-experimental Designs for Research* (pp. 171–246). Boston: Houghton Mifflin.

Canadian Institutes of Health Research, Natural Sciences and Engineering Research Council of Canada, and Social Sciences and Humanities Research Council of Canada (2010) Research involving the First Nations, Inuit, and Métis Peoples of Canada. In *Tri-Council Policy Statement: Ethical Conduct for Research Involving Humans*, December. Retrieved from http://www.pre.ethics.gc.ca/eng/policy-politique/initiatives/tcps2-eptc2/chapter9-chapitre9/#toc09-1 (7 February 2013).

Charmaz, K. (2000) Grounded theory: objectionist and constructionist methods. In N.K. Denzin and Y.S. Lincoln (eds), *Handbook of Qualitative Research*, 2nd edition. Thousand Oaks, CA: Sage.

Clarke, J. (2013) Constructing understandings of loss: parents' perspectives following the death of their baby. PhD thesis, University of Sydney.

Cohen, J. (1988) *Statistical Power Analysis for the Behavioral Sciences*, 2nd edition. Hillsdale, NJ: Lawrence Erlbaum Associates.

Cole, A.L. and Knowles, J.G. (2011) Drawing on the arts, transforming research: possibilities of arts informed perspectives. In L. Markauskaite, P. Freebody and J. Irwin (eds), *Methodological Choice and Design: Scholarship, Policy and Practice in Social and Educational Research*. Dordrecht: Springer.

Commission on the Social Determinants of Health (2008) *Closing the Gap in a Generation: Health Equity through Action on the Social Determinants of Health*, Final Report of the Commission on Social Determinants of Health. Geneva: World Health Organization.

Couturier, Y., Gagnon, D., Carrier, S. and Etheridge, F. (2008) The interdisciplinary condition of work in relational professions of the health and social care field: a theoretical standpoint. *Journal of Interprofessional Care*, 22(4): 341–351.

D'Cruz, H. and Jones, M. (2004) *Social Work Research in Practice*. London: Sage.

D'Cruz, H. and Jones, M. (2014) *Social Work Research in Practice: Ethical and Political Contexts*, 2nd edition. London: Sage.

Davys, A. and Beddoe, L. (2010) *Best Practice in Professional Supervision: A Guide for the Helping Professions*. London: Jessica Kingsley.

Denicolo, P. (2003) Assessing the PhD: a constructive view of criteria. *Quality Assurance in Education*, 11(2): 84–91.

Denscombe, M. (2002) *Ground Rules for Good Research: A 10 Point Guide for Social Research.* Buckingham: Open University Press.

Denzin, N.K. (1989) *Interpretative Biography.* London/Thousand Oaks: Sage.

Department for Communities and Local Government (2011a) *The English Indices of Deprivation, 2010: Neighbourhoods Statistical Release.* Available online at http://bit.ly/1wMNfZu.

Department for Communities and Local Government (2011b) *The English Indices of Deprivation, 2010: Technical Report.* London: DCLG.

Department for Education (2011) *An Action Plan for Adoption: Tackling Delay.* London: Department for Education.

Department for Education (2012) *Children looked after in England (including adoption and care leavers),* SFR 20/2012. Available online at www.education.gov.uk/researchandstatistics/statistics/allstatistics/a00213762/children-looked-after-las-england.

Department of Health (2011) *Improving Direct Payment Delivery: Think Local, Act Personal.* London: Department of Health.

Dodd, S.-J. and Epstein, I. (2012) *Practice-Based Research in Social Work: A Guide for Reluctant Researchers.* New York: Routledge.

Drury Hudson, J. (1997) A model for professional knowledge for social work. *Australian Social Work,* 50(3): 35–44.

Dunne, J. (2005) An intricate fabric: understanding the rationality of practice. *Pedagogy, Culture and Society,* 13(3): 367–389.

Epstein, I. (2001) Using available clinical information in practice-based research: mining for silver while dreaming of gold. In I. Epstein and S. Blumenfield (eds), *Clinical Data-Mining in Practice-Based Research: Social Work in Hospital Settings.* Binghamton, NY: Haworth Press.

Epstein, I. (2009) Promoting harmony where there is commonly conflict: evidence-informed practice as an integrative strategy. *Social Work in Health Care,* 48(3): 216–231.

Epstein, I. (2010) *Clinical Data-Mining: Integrating Practice and Research.* New York: Oxford University Press.

Epstein, I. (2012) The practitioner as researcher: evidence-informed practice as an integrative strategy. Lecture given at University of Sydney, 12 May, unpublished.

Epstein, I. and Blumenfield, S. (eds) (2001) *Clinical Data-Mining in Practice-Based Research: Social Work in Hospital Settings.* Binghamton NY: Haworth Press.

Fawcett, B. (2000) *Feminist Perspectives on Disability.* Harlow: Prentice Hall.

Fawcett, B., Featherstone, B., Fook, J. and Rossiter, A. (eds) (2000) *Practice and Research in Social Work: Postmodern and Feminist Perspectives.* London: Routledge.

Fawcett, B., Goodwin, S. and Phillips, R. (2011) Challenges and futures for social work and social policy research methods. In L. Markauskaite, P. Freebody and J. Irwin (eds), *Methodological Choice and Design: Scholarship, Policy and Practice in Social and Educational Research.* Dordrecht: Springer.

Fawcett, B., Goodwin, S., Meagher, G. and Phillips, R. (2010) *Social Policy for Social Change*. Melbourne: Palgrave Macmillan.

Featherstone, B. and Fawcett, B. (1995) Oh no! Not more isms: feminism, postmodernism, poststructuralism and social work education. *Social Work Education*, 14(3): 25–43.

Finch, J. (1986) *Research and Policy: The Use of Qualitative Methods in Social and Educational Research*. Lewes: Falmer.

Flax, J. (1992) The end of innocence. In J. Butler and J. Scott (eds), *Feminists Theorise the Political*. London: Routledge.

Fook, J. (2002) Critical deconstruction and reconstruction. In *Social Work Critical Theory and Practice*. London: Sage.

Fook, J. and Gardner, F. (2007) *Practising Critical Reflection: A Resource Handbook*. Maidenhead: McGraw-Hill/Open University Press.

Fook, J., White, S. and Gardner, F. (2006) Critical reflection: a review of contemporary literature and understandings. In S. White, J. Fook and F. Gardner (eds), *Critical Reflection in Health and Social Care*. Maidenhead: McGraw-Hill/Open University Press.

Forder, J., Jones, K., Glendinning, C., Caiels, J., Welch, E., Baxter, K., et al. (2012) *Evaluation of the Personal Health Budget Pilot Programme*, Discussion Paper 2840_2. London: Department of Health.

Foucault, M. (1977) *Discipline and Punish*. London: Penguin.

Foucault, M. (1980) *Michel Foucault: Power/Knowledge: Selected Interviews and Other Writings 1972–1977 by Michel Foucault*, edited by C. Gorden. Hemel Hempstead: Harvester Wheatsheaf.

Foucault, M. (1981a) *The History of Sexuality, Volume One: An Introduction*. Harmondsworth: Penguin.

Foucault, M. (1981b) Question of method: an interview with Michel Foucault. *Ideology and Consciousness*, 8: 1–14.

Fouché, C. and Light, G. (2011) An invitation to dialogue: 'The world café' in social work research. *Qualitative Social Work*, 10(1): 28–48.

Fouché, C. and Lunt, N. (2009) Using groups to advance social work practice-based research. *Social Work with Groups*, 32(1–2): 47–63.

Fraser, N. (1990) Struggle over needs: outline of a socialist-feminist critical theory of late-capitalist political culture. In L. Gordon (ed.), *Women, the State, and Welfare*. Madison: University of Wisconsin Press.

Fraser, N. and Nicholson, L. (1993) Social criticism without philosophy: an encounter between feminism and postmodernism. In M. Docherty (ed.), *Postmodernism: A Reader*. Hemel Hempstead: Harvester Wheatsheaf.

Gabriel, M. (2010) Writing up research. In M. Walter (ed.), *Social Research Methods*, 2nd edition (pp. 439–471). South Melbourne: Oxford University Press.

Gardner, F. (2006) Using critical reflection in research and evaluation. In S. White, J. Fook and F. Gardner (eds), *Critical Reflection in Health and Social Care*. Maidenhead: Open University Press.

Garfinkel, H. (1967) *Studies in Ethnomethodology*. Englewood Cliffs, NJ: Prentice Hall.

Giles, R., Epstein, I. and Vertigan, A. (eds) (2011) *Clinical Data Mining in an Allied Health Organization: A Real World Experience*. Sydney: Sydney University Press.

Giles, R., Irwin, J., Lynch, D. and Waugh, F. (2010) *In the Field: From Learning to Practice*. South Melbourne: Oxford University Press.

Gilligan, C. (1982) *In a Different Voice: Psychological Theory and Women's Development*. Cambridge, MA: Harvard University Press.

Glannon, W. (2002) Introduction to the history, theory and methods of biomedical ethics. In W. Glannon (ed.), *Contemporary Readings in Biomedical Ethics* (pp. 1–33). Fort Worth, TX: Harcourt College Publishers.

Glasby, J. (2012) *Healthy Choice? The National Evaluation of Personal Budgets: Policy Research Programme Proposal*. London: Department of Health.

Glaser, B.G. and Strauss, A.L. (1967) *The Discovery of Grounded Theory Analysis*. Chicago: Aldine.

Gorard, S. (2002) Fostering scepticism: the importance of warranting claims. *Evaluation and Research in Education*, 16(3): 136–149.

Graham, I., Logan, J., Harrison, M., Straus, S., Tetroe, J., Caswell, W. and Robinson, N. (2006) Lost in knowledge translations: time for a map? *Journal of Continuing Education in the Health Professions*, 26(1): 13–24.

Gray, M. (2010) Moral sources and emergent ethical theories in social work. *British Journal of Social Work*, 40: 1794–1811.

Grbich, C. (2004) *New Approaches in Social Research*. London: Sage.

Grbich, C. (2007) *Qualitative Data Analysis: An Introduction*. London: Sage.

Green, B. (2009) *Understanding and Researching Professional Practice*. Rotterdam: Sense.

Green, J.L., Camilli, G. and Elmore, P.B. (eds) (2006) *Handbook of Complementary Methods in Education Research*. Chicago: Routledge.

Guba, E.G. (1981) Criteria for assessing the trustworthiness of naturalistic inquiries. *Educational Resources Information Center Annual Review Paper*, 29: 75–91.

Guba, E.G. and Lincoln, Y.S. (2000) Paradigmatic controversies, contradictions and emerging confluences. In N.K. Denzin and Y.S. Lincoln (eds), *Handbook of Qualitative Research*. Thousand Oaks, CA: Sage.

Habibis, D. (2010) Ethics and social research. In M. Walter (ed.), *Social Research Methods* (pp. 89–122). South Melbourne: Oxford University Press.

Hakim, C. (2000) *Research Design*, 2nd edition. Abingdon: Taylor and Francis.

Hall, D. and Hall, I. (1996) *Practical Social Research*. Basingstoke: Macmillan.

Harris-Roxas, B. and Harris, E. (2011) Differing forms, differing purposes: a typology of health impact assessment. *Environmental Impact Assessment Review*, 31: 396–403.

Hart, C. (1999) *Doing a Literature Review: Releasing the Social Science Imagination*. London: Sage.

Health Research Council of New Zealand (2008) *Guidelines for Researchers on Health Research Involving Māori*. Auckland: Health Research Council of New Zealand.

Heidegger, M. (1993/1998) *Basic Writings* (D. Farrell Krell, trans.). New York: HarperCollins.

Henderson, J., Smith, C., Smith, D., Barnett, C., Haskins, R. and Rutledge, K. (2011) A data-mining medley for physiotherapists: cleaning up data codes, evaluating service and improving client outcomes. In R. Giles, I. Epstein and A. Vertigan (eds), *Clinical Data Mining in an Allied Health Organization: A Real World Experience*. Sydney: Sydney University Press.

Heron, J. and Reason, P. (1997) A participatory inquiry paradigm. *Qualitative Inquiry*, 3: 274–294.

Hershock, P. (2000) Dramatic intervention: human rights from a Buddhist perspective. *Philosophy East and West*, 50(1): 9–33.

Higgins, J.P.T. and Green, S. (eds) (2011) *Cochrane Handbook for Systematic Reviews of Interventions,* Version 5.1.0. Cochrane Collaboration. Available from www.cochrane-handbook.org.

Hobbs, K. (2008) Psychosocial distress and cervical cancer. *Cancer Forum*, 32(2): 89–92.

Hodgkinson, K., Butow, P., Fuchs, A., Hunt, G., Stenlake, A., Hobbs, K., et al. (2006) Long-term survival from gynecological cancer: psychosocial outcomes, supportive care needs and positive outcomes. *Gynecologic Oncology*, 104: 381–389.

Hodgkinson, K., Butow, P., Hobbs, K. and Wain, G. (2007a) After cancer: the unmet supportive care needs of survivors and their partners. *Journal of Psychosocial Oncology*, 25(4): 89–104.

Hodgkinson, K., Butow, P., Hobbs, K., Hunt, G., Lo, S. and Wain, G. (2007b) Assessing unmet supportive care needs in partners of cancer survivors: the development and evaluation of the Cancer Survivors' Partners Unmet Needs Measure (CaSPUN). *Psycho-Oncology*, 16: 805–813.

Howell, K. (2013) *An Introduction to the Philosophy of Methodology.* London: Sage.

Hugman, R. (2005) *New Approaches in Ethics for the Caring Professions.* Basingstoke: Palgrave Macmillan.

Hugman, R., Pittaway, E. and Bartolomei, L. (2011) When 'do no harm' is not enough: the ethics of research with refugees and other vulnerable groups. *British Journal of Social Work*, 41(7): 1271–1287.

Humphrey, A. (2005) SWOT analysis for management consulting. *SRI Alumni Newsletter (SRI International)*.

Ife, J. (1997) *Rethinking Social Work: Towards Critical Practice.* Melbourne: Longman.

Ife, J. (2008) *Human Rights and Social Work: Towards Rights-Based Practice,* revised edition. Port Melbourne: Cambridge University Press.

Jantsch, E. (1971) Inter- and transdisciplinary university: a systems approach to education and innovation. *Ekistics*, 32: 430–437.

Joubert, L. (2006) Academic-practice partnerships in practice research: a cultural shift for health social workers. *Social Work in Health Care*, 43(2/3): 151–162.

Kadushin, A. (1985) *Supervision in Social Work*, 2nd edition. New York: Columbia University Press.

Kaiser, K. (2009) Protecting respondent confidentiality in qualitative research. *Qualitative Health Research*, 19(11): 1632–1641.

Kemmis, S. (2005) Knowing practice: searching for saliences. *Pedagogy, Culture and Society*, 13(3): 391–426.

Kemmis, S. (2009) Understanding professional practice: a synoptic framework. In B. Green (ed.), *Understanding and Researching Professional Practice* (pp. 19–39). Rotterdam: Sense.

Kendrick, D., Elkan, R., Hewitt, M., Dewey, M., Blair, M., Robinson, J., et al. (2000) Does home visiting improve parenting and the quality of the home environment? A systematic review and meta analysis. *Archives of Disease in Childhood*, 82: 443–451.

Kettner, P., Moroney, R. and Martin, L. (1990) *Designing and Managing Programs*. Newbury Park, CA: Sage

Kierkegaard, S. (1985) *Fear and Trembling* (A. Hannay, trans.). London: Penguin.

Klein, J. (1996) *Crossing Boundaries: Knowledge, Disciplinarities, and Interdisciplinarities*. Charlottseville: University Press of Virginia.

Krefting, L. (1991) Rigor in qualitative research: the assessment of trustworthiness. *American Journal of Occupational Therapy*, 45(3): 214–222.

Krieger, N., Northridge, M., Gruskin, S., Quinn, M., Kriebel, D., Davey Smith, G., et al. (2003) Assessing health impact assessment: multidisciplinary and international perspectives. *Journal of Epidemiology and Community Health*, 57(9): 659–662.

Krueger, R.A. (1994) *Focus Groups: A Practical Guide for Applied Research*. London: Sage.

Kushner, S. (2000) *Personalizing Evaluation*. London: Sage.

Lincoln, Y.S. and Guba, E.G. (1985) *Naturalistic Inquiry*. Beverly Hills, CA: Sage.

Loupis, Y. (2013) Family conferences in stroke rehabilitation: a literature review. *Journal of Stroke and Cerebrovascular Diseases*, 22(6): 883–893.

Love, K., Pritchard, C., Maguire, K., McCarthy, A. and Paddock, P. (2005) Qualitative and quantitative approaches to health impact assessment: an analysis of the political and philosophical milieu of the multi-method approach. *Critical Public Health*, 15(3): 275–289.

Lyotard, J-F. (1992) *The Postmodern Explained to Children: Corrrespondence 1982–1985* (D. Barry et al., trans.; J. Pefanis & M. Thomas, eds). Sydney: Power Publications.

Macdonald, G. (2001) *Effective Interventions for Child Abuse and Neglect: An Evidence-Based Approach to Planning and Evaluating Interventions*. Chichester: Wiley.

Macnaghten, P. (1993) Discourses of nature: argumentation and power. In E. Burman and I. Parker (eds), *Discourse Analytic Research: Repetoires and Readings of Texts in Action*. London: Sage.

Marshall, C. and Rossman, G.B. (1995) *Designing Qualitative Research*. London: Sage.

Mason, J. (2002) *Qualitative Researching*, 2nd edition. London: Sage.

McCune, V. and Entwistle, N. (2011) Cultivating the disposition to understand in 21st century university education. *Learning and Individual Differences*, 21: 303–310.

Mezirow, J. (2000) *Learning as Transformation: Critical Perspectives in a Theory in Progress*. San Francisco: Jossey-Bass.

Mickan, S. and Rodger, S. (2005) Effective health care teams: a model of six characteristics developed from shared perceptions. *Journal of Interprofessional Care*, 19(4): 358–370.

Mill, J.S. (1987) *Utilitarianism and Other Essays*. London: Penguin.

Miller, S., Maguire, L.K. and Macdonald, G. (2012) Home-based child development interventions for preschool children from socially disadvantaged families. *Campbell Systematic Reviews 2012*: 1. DOI: 10.4073/csr.2012.1. Available at http://bit.ly/1xHvJEZ.

Moher, D., Hopewell, S., Schulz, K.F., Montori, V., Gøtzsche, P.C., Devereaux, P.J., et al. for the CONSORT Group (2010) CONSORT 2010 explanation and elaboration: updated guidelines for reporting parallel group randomised trial. *British Medical Journal*, 340: c869.

Moher, D., Liberati, A., Tetzlaff, J., Altman, D.G. and the PRISMA Group (2009) *Preferred Reporting Items for Systematic Reviews and Meta-Analyses: The PRISMA Statement*. PLoS Medicine 6(7): e1000097. Retrieved from http://www.prisma-statement.org (9 April 2014).

Moore, M., Beazley, S. and Maelzer, J. (1998) *Researching Disability Issues*. Buckingham: Open University Press.

Morgan, D.L. (1997) *Focus Groups as Qualitative Research*. London: Sage.

Morley, C. (2011) Some methodological and ethical tensions in using critical reflection as a research methodology. In J. Fook and F. Gardner (eds), *Critical Reflection in Context: Applications in Health and Social Care*. Oxon: Routledge.

National Association of Social Workers (2008) Code of Ethics of the National Association of Social Workers. Retrieved from http://www.socialworkers.org/pubs/code/default.asp (13 February 2013).

National Health and Medical Research Foundation (2003) *Values and Ethics – Guidelines for Ethical Conduct in Aboriginal and Torres Strait Islander Health Research*. Retrieved from http://www.nhmrc.gov.au/guidelines/publications/e52 (8 February 2013).

Nicholas, J., Stevens, L., Briggs, L. and Wood, L. (2013) *Children's Food Trust: Eat Better Do Better, Research Report*. Sheffield: Children's Food Trust.

Noddings, N. (1984) *Caring: A Feminine Approach to Ethics and Moral Education*. Berkeley: University of California Press.

O'Hara, A. (2011) Introduction to working with groups. In A. O'Hara and R. Pockett (eds), *Skills for Human Service Practice: Working with Individuals, Groups and Communities* (pp. 226–255). South Melbourne: Oxford University Press.

O'Sullivan, E. (1999) *Transformative Learning: Educational Vision for the 21st Century*. Toronto: University of Toronto Press.

Olssen, M. and Peters, M.A. (2005) Neoliberalism, higher education and the knowledge economy: from the free market to knowledge capitalism. *Journal of Education Policy*, 20(3): 313–335.

Opie, A. (1992) Qualitative research, appropriation of the 'other' and empowerment. *Feminist Review*, 40/42: 52–69.

Patrick, J. (1973) *A Glasgow Gang Observed*. London: Wyre-Methuen.

Pawson, R., Boaz, A., Grayson, L., Long, A. and Barnes, C. (2003) *Types and Quality of Knowledge in Social Care*. London: SCIE.

Pawson, R., Greenhalgh T., Harvey, G. and Walshe, K. (2005) Realist review – a new method of systematic review designed for complex policy interventions. *Journal of Health Services Research & Policy*, 10(1 Supplement): 21–34.

Payne, C. (2012) *The Consumer, Credit and Neoliberalism: Governing the Modern Economy*. Abingdon: Routledge.

Pittaway, E., Bartolomei, L. and Hugman, R. (2010) 'Stop stealing our stories': the ethics of research with vulnerable groups. *Journal of Human Rights Practice*, 2(2): 229–251.

Plath, D. (2006) Evidence-based practice: current issue and future directions. *Australian Social Work*, 59(1): 56–72.

Pockett, R. (2009) Data-mining 'victim of crime' presentations in hospital emergency departments: a research tool with wider significance. In P. Bywaters, E. McLeod and L. Napier (eds), *Social Work and Global Health Inequalities: Practice and Policy Developments*. Bristol: Policy Press.

Pockett, R., Walker, E. and Dave, K. (2010) 'Last orders': dying in a hospital setting. *Australian Social Work*, 63(3): 250–265.

Polanyi, M. (1967) *The Tacit Dimension*. London: Routledge & Kegan Paul.

Poore, M. (2014) *Studying and Researching with Social Media*. London: Sage.

Posavac, E. and Carey, R. (1980) *Program Evaluation*. Englewood Cliffs, NJ: Prentice Hall.

Potter, J. and Wetherell, M. (1987) *Discourse and Social Psychology*. London: Sage.

Potter, J. and Wetherell, M. (1994) Analysing discourse. In A. Bryman and R.G. Burgess (eds), *Analysing Qualitative Data*. London: Routledge.

Prasad, M. (2006) *The Rise of Neoliberal Economic Policies in Britain, France, Germany and the United States*. Chicago: University of Chicago Press.

Pritchard, P. (1995) Learning how to work effectively in teams. In P. Owens, J. Carrier and J. Horder (eds), *Interprofessional Issues in Community and Primary Health Care*. Basingstoke: Macmillan.

Rawsthorne, M. and Hoffman, S. (2010) Supporting safe and healthy relationship choices: a peer education approach. *Women Against Violence*, 22: 28–40.

Reid, K. (1997) *Social Work Practice with Groups: A Clinical Perspective*. Pacific Grove, CA: Brooks/Cole.

Ritchie, J. and Spencer, I. (1994) Qualitative data analysis for applied research. In A. Bryman and R.G. Burgess (eds), *Analyzing Qualitative Data*. London: Routledge.

Rosenthal, G. (1990) The structure and 'gestalt' of autobiographies and its methodological consequences. Paper presented at the XIIth World Congress of Sociology, Madrid.

Rosenthal, G. (1993) Reconstruction of life stories. In R. Josselson and A. Lieblich (eds), *The Narrative Study of Lives*, Vol. 1. Newbury Park, CA: Sage.

Rossi, P. and Freeman, H. (1982) *Evaluation*, 2nd edition. Beverly Hills, CA: Sage.

Rutter, D., Francis, J., Coren, E. and Fisher, M. (2013) *SCIE Systematic Research Reviews: Guidelines*, 2nd edition. London: SCIE. Available at www.scie.org.uk.

Sapsford, R. and Jupp, V. (eds) (2006) *Data Collection and Analysis*. London: Sage.

Schatzki, T. (2001) Practice theory. In T.R. Schatzki, K. Knorr-Cetina and E. von Savigny (eds), *The Practice Turn in Contemporary Theory*. London: Routledge.

Schiller, L.Y. (1997) Rethinking stages of development in women's groups: implications for practice. *Social Work with Groups*, 20: 3–19.

Schön, D. (1983) *The Reflective Practitioner: How Professionals Think in Action*. New York: Basic Books/HarperCollins.

Schön, D. (1987) *Educating the Reflective Practitioner*. San Francisco: Jossey-Bass.

Sharland, E. and Taylor, I. (2006) Social care research: a suitable case for systematic review? *Evidence & Policy*, 2(4): 503–523.

Shaw, I. and Lunt, N. (2011) Navigating practitioner research. *British Journal of Social Work*, 41(8): 1548–1565.

Shaw, I. and Lunt, N. (2012) Constructing practitioner research. *Social Work Research*, 36(3): 197–208.

Silverman, D. (2000) *Doing Qualitative Research: A Practical Handbook*. London: Sage.

Silverman, D. (ed.) (2004) *Qualitative Research: Theory, Method and Practice*. London: Sage.

Silverman, D. (2013) *Doing Qualitative Research: A Practical Handbook*, 4th edition. London: Sage.

Simmonds, D., Porter, J., O'Rourke, P., West, L., Tangey, A. and Holland, C. (2010) 'You can tell us your things and we'll teach you ours': a 'two ways' approach to improving antenatal education for Ngaanyatjarra women. *Aboriginal and Islander Health Worker Journal*, 34(2): 10–14.

Slasberg, C., Beresford, P. and Schofield, P. (2012) How self-directed support is failing to deliver personal budgets and personalization. *Research, Policy and Planning*, 29(3): 161–177.

Smith, D. (1990) *Texts, Facts and Femininity: Exploring the Relations of Ruling*. London: Routledge.

Stake, R. (1967) The countenance of educational evaluation. *Teachers College Record*, 68(7): 523–540.

Stevenson, M. (2012) Inclusive researching and circles of support. PhD thesis, University of Sydney.

Strauss, A. and Corbin, J. (2000) *Basics of Qualitative Research: Grounded Theory Procedures and Techniques*. Thousand Oaks, CA: Sage.

Suchman, E. (1967) *Evaluative Research*. New York: Russell Sage.

Taylor, C. (2006) Practising reflexivity: narrative, reflection and the moral order. In S. White, J. Fook and F. Gardner (eds), *Critical Reflection in Health and Social Care*. Maidenhead: Open University Press.

Taylor, C. and White, S. (2000) *Practising Reflexivity in Health and Welfare: Making Knowledge*. Buckingham: Open University Press.

Taylor, C. and White, S. (2006) Knowledge and reasoning in social work: educating for humane judgement. *British Journal of Social Work*, 36: 937–954.

Tolich, M. (2004) Internal confidentiality: when confidentiality assurances fail relational informants. *Qualitative Sociology*, 27: 101–106.

Turnbull, C. and Osborn, D.A. (2012) Home visits during pregnancy and after birth for women with an alcohol or drug problem. *Cochrane Database of Systematic Reviews* 2012, Issue 1. Art. No.: CD004456. DOI: 10.1002/14651858.CD004456. pub3.

Uggerhøj, L. (2011) Theorizing practice research in social work. *Social Work and Social Sciences Review*, 15(1): 49–73.

United Nations High Commission for Human Rights (1966) International Covenant on Civil and Political Rights. Retrieved from http://www2.ohchr.org/english/law/ccpr.htm (13 February 2013).

US Department of Health and Human Services (1949) *Trials of War Criminals before the Nuremberg Military Tribunals under Control Council Law No. 10*, Vol. 2, pp. 181–182. Washington, DC: US Government Printing Office. http://www.hhs.gov/ohrp/archive/nurcode.html.

Vinson, T. (2007) *Dropping off the Edge: The Distribution of Disadvantage in Australia. A Report of Jesuit Social Services and Catholic Social Services Australia*. Jesuit Social Services/Catholic Social Services Australia.

Weber, Z. and Pockett, R. (2011a) Professional values and ethical practice. In A. O'Hara and R. Pockett (eds), *Skills for Human Service Practice: Working with Individuals, Groups and Communities* (pp. 20–42). South Melbourne: Oxford University Press.

Weber, Z. and Pockett, R. (2011b) Working effectively in teams. In A. O'Hara and R. Pockett (eds), *Skills for Human Service Practice: Working with Individuals, Groups and Communities* (pp. 274–295). South Melbourne: Oxford University Press.

Weedon, C. (1987) *Feminist Practice and Poststructuralist Theory*. Oxford: Blackwell.

White, P. (2009) *Developing Research Questions: A Guide for Social Scientists*. Basingstoke, Hampshire: Palgrave Macmillan.

White, R. (2010) Doing evaluation research. In M. Walter (ed.), *Social Research Methods*, 2nd Edition. South Melbourne: Oxford University Press.

Wilkinson, R. and Pickett, K. (2010) *The Spirit Level: Why Equality is Better for Everyone*. London: Penguin.

Williams, F. (1994) Michele Barrett: from Marxist to poststructural feminism. In V. George and R. Page (eds), *Modern Thinkers on Welfare*. Hemel Hempstead: Harvester Wheatsheaf.

Williams, F. (1996) Postmodernism, feminism and the question of difference. In N. Parton (ed.), *Social Theory, Social Change and Social Work*. London: Routledge.

Williams, M. and May, T. (1996) *Introduction to the Philosophy of Social Research*. London: UCL Press.

World Medical Association (1964) *Declaration of Helsinki: Ethical Principles for Medical Research Involving Human Subjects*. Retrieved from http://www.wma.net/en/30publications/10policies/b3/index.html (2 February 2011).

Wright, D.B. (1997) *Understanding Statistics*. London: Sage.

Yegidis, B. and Weinbach, R. (2008) *Research Methods for Social Workers*, 6th edition. Boston: Allyn and Bacon.

Zief, S.G., Lauver, S. and Maynard, R.A. (2006) *Impacts of After-School Programs on Student Outcomes: A Systematic Review*. Campbell Collaboration. Available at: http://campbellcollaboration.org/lib/project/12/ (10 April 2014).

Zilberfein, F., Hutson, C., Snyder, S. and Epstein, I. (2001) Social work practice with pre- and post-liver transplant patients: a retrospective self-study. *Social Work in Health Care*, 33(3/4): 91–104.

Index

Figures and Tables are indicated by page numbers printed in bold.